The Punic Wars

A Captivating Guide to the First, Second, and Third Punic Wars Between Rome and Carthage, Including the Rise and Fall of Hannibal Barca

Contents

Introduction

The Punic Wars between 264 BCE and 146 BCE were a series of wars fought between the armies of ancient Carthage and Rome. In the years before the battles broke out, Carthage had risen from a small port community to the Mediterranean region's richest and most powerful city. Carthage had a powerful navy, a mercenary army, and ample resources to act as an authority in trade and politics. As such, Carthage prohibited Roman trade in the Western Mediterranean through an agreement with what was then just a small city called Rome. Without an organized military, Rome had little choice but to abide by the treaty.

As history shows, however, Rome didn't stay small and insignificant for long. As its size and power grew, so too did Rome's desire to fight back against its Carthaginian oppressors: so followed the three Punic Wars. At the start of the conflict, Carthage dominated the Mediterranean. By the end of the wars, Rome had not only conquered Carthage but become the strongest society in the Western Mediterranean. It was a formative period for the Roman Republic and one that would eventually lead Rome to form its own empire.

The loosely-knit Carthaginian Empire is synonymous with the Punic Empire, as the two were one and the same. The Punic Wars, therefore, are interchangeable with the Carthaginian Wars, as it simply depends on which name is preferred. The following is a breakdown of the years in which the First, Second, and Third Punic Wars took place:

First Punic War: 264-241 BCE

Second Punic War: 218-201 BCE

Third Punic War: 149-146 BCE

To track the progress of the wars in a straightforward manner, this book is divided into chapters based on the year in which a battle or succession of battles took place. The most significant battles, treaties, and turning points of all three wars are included here, although some events with few records have been excluded.

Chapter One – The Phoenicians and Carthage

The history of the Carthaginian Empire begins with the Phoenicians, an ancient people with origins in the region of modern Syria, Lebanon, and Israel. Theirs was a strong maritime society known for its large horse-headed ships fashioned in deference to the sea god, Yam (also Yamm). The capital city of the Phoenicians was created in the 3rd millennium BCE at Tyre, in today's Lebanon, and it was here that the society's most famous industry was founded: dyeing textiles a rich purple color for the Mesopotamian royalty.

In fact, the purple dye manufactured in Tyre gave the people their name: Phoenicians. The name is derived from the Greek PHOINIKES, WHICH MEANT "Tyrian Purple."[1] According to the Greek historian Herodotus, the dye stained the skin of the workers, and so the Greeks called them "Purple People."[2]

The Phoenician society was complex and multifaceted, characterized by great intelligence, trade, literature, and art. Herodotus attributes the foundation of the Greek alphabet to that of the Phoenicians, with

---

[1] Mark, Joshua J. "Phoenicia." *Ancient History Encyclopedia.* Web. 2018.

[2] Ibid.

the latter comprising the basis of most western languages today. Using that very alphabet, Phoenicians wrote some of the first books in the world on papyrus made in their own city of Gebal. Gebal, known as "Byblos" or "the books" to the Greeks, lent its name permanently to the Judeo-Christian Bible.

Through successful trade and economic prosperity, these people founded several city-states along the rim of the Mediterranean Sea. One such city was Carthage, founded in modern Tunisia at some point between 813 and 825 BCE.[3]

The Phoenician culture blossomed for thousands of years, but it was an attractive target to leaders of neighboring societies. In 575 BCE, the Babylonian King Nebuchadnezzar set his sights on the prosperous island city of Tyre, eventually subduing it as part of the Persian Empire by forcing it to pay a tribute. Having been subjugated in this way, Tyre could no longer support its own colonies with warships and fighting men when the need arose. Nevertheless, it remained an important city unto itself and to the Persians until falling victim to another great army.

The Macedonian Emperor Alexander the Great lay siege to Tyre in 332 BCE as part of his campaign to conquer the Persian Empire.[4] The city, nearly impossible to penetrate due to its location on an island surrounded by fortifications said to be 150 feet high, had taken thirteen years for Nebuchadnezzar to conquer.[5] Foreseeing the advances of Alexander, rulers in Tyre sent women and children to Carthage and prepared to weather the siege confidently.

Alexander, for his part, took tremendous time and care in mounting his attack. His men built a large causeway from the mainland to the island, and though his army's advance was halted spectacularly by

---

[3] "Carthage." *Livius*. Web.

[4] Grant. "Alexander's Seige of Tyre." *Ancient History Encyclopedia*. 2011.

[5] Ibid.

the Tyrians, six months later, the Macedonian emperor made his way into the island city and destroyed much of what he found there. Remarkably, the city of Tyre survived, though no longer as an island thanks to further construction to strengthen and widen Alexander's causeway. Alive though it was, Tyre was even further removed from its Phoenician heritage.

Carthage became the leader of the Phoenician colonies in the west after the fall of its mother-city, and afterward founded a powerful empire of its own.[6] For centuries, the Carthaginian Empire fought against that of the Greeks, as was logistically natural given their respective locations on opposite shores of the Mediterranean Sea. The two cultures endured times of war, times of peace, and—most often—times of trade, and thereby knew a great deal about one another. The Macedonian philosopher Aristotle of Stagira wrote a description of the constitution of Carthage sometime in the 4th century BCE:

> The Carthaginians are considered to have an excellent form of government, which differs from that of any other state in several respects, though it is in some very like the Spartan. Indeed, the Spartan, Cretan, and Carthaginian states closely resemble one another and are very different from any others.
>
> Many of the Carthaginian institutions are excellent. The superiority of their constitution is proved by the fact that the common people remain loyal to it. The Carthaginians have never had any rebellion worth speaking of, and have never been under the rule of a tyrant.
>
> They ... have their kings and their *Gerousia*, or council of elders, who correspond to the kings and elders of Sparta. Their kings, unlike the Spartan, are not always of the same family, nor that an ordinary one, but if there is some

---

[6] Ibid.

distinguished family they are selected out of it and not appointed by seniority.

The government of the Carthaginians is oligarchic, but they successfully escape the evils of oligarchy by enriching one portion of the people after another by sending them to their colonies. This is their panacea and the means by which they give stability to the state. Accident favors them, but the legislator should be able to provide against revolution without trusting to accidents. As things are, if any misfortune occurred, and the bulk of the subjects revolted, there would be no way of restoring peace by legal methods.[7]

Though it could not be considered a primarily warlike empire like that of Alexander the Great, the Carthaginian Empire was not in search of endless peace, either. Kings of Carthage and its Phoenician allies greatly disliked the Greeks and often worked together to beat the latter back from their home shores. By 220 BCE, the Carthaginian Empire ruled over the entire southwestern length of the Mediterranean Sea, as well as the northern lengths as far as modern Spain. To the east lay the Ptolemaic Empire, centered on the city of Alexandria in Egypt; to the north lay the greatly-reduced Macedonian/Greek Empires under the collaborative Hellenistic treaty, plus the newly-powerful Roman Empire.

As Carthage's Greek enemies lost ground to the Romans, the former found themselves with a new foe across the sea.

---

[7] From "Carthage's Constitution." *Livius.* Web.

Chapter Two – The Romans

Ancient Greece flourished during the first millennium BCE, reaching a pinnacle of culture and influence during the 5th century BCE. Like its neighboring Mediterranean societies, Greece was a colonial collection of city-states that reached across the sea into ancient Italy. These early Italian colonies were often referred to as "Greater Greece." It is for this reason that the Roman Republic, as it began to grow and enact its own authority over Italy, had a very distinct Grecian style to it. Romans created their own versions of the Greek gods, Greek government, and Greek military. For this reason, the closely connected societies are collectively known as the Greco-Roman civilization.

By the 4th century BCE, the city of Rome had thrown off the rule of kings and established itself as a republic, complete with elected senators.[8] With a government at the helm, Rome made great strides to expand its territory, first in Latium and then in all Italy. Romans, rising in prosperity and fame for their pursuit of military gains as well as philosophical knowledge, continued to emulate their Greek

---

[8] "Roman Republic." *Encyclopaedia Britannica*. Web.

neighbors to a great degree. Generally making enemies only to acquire land, the Roman Republic became an accepted superpower of the Mediterranean. Unlike most other superpowers, however, the Romans believed that theirs was the best society due not only to their style of warfare but also their form of democratic government and pursuit of higher education.

After centuries of domination under the tyranny of kings, Romans believed fervently in their political system. The last thing they would allow was a single person to grip the reigns of authority over the entire city and its collective communities. To fairly distribute power, the republicans arranged a system by which male members of the noble Roman families—called patricians—were expected to serve in political office for at least a term. Among the serving patricians, there were to be regular elections for a set of two consuls who would rule together over the republic for a pre-set term. Most Roman citizens—lacking noble birth and called plebeians—had no right to vote or serve in government.

The two elected consuls, whose ultimate power essentially replaced that of the king, were generals whose task was to lead Rome's armies in war. As the republic expanded, it became customary for one consul to rule at home, while the second ruled the colonies. The purpose of electing two consuls at one time was simple: they would keep one another in check so that their policies would ideally be balanced. At times of war, when there was ruled to be a military emergency, a dictator would be appointed instead of the consuls. The dictator had free reign to do what was necessary to protect Rome without lengthy discussion and voting, but he could only hold this office for six months.

Though the later Roman Empire would become one of the most literate and well-written societies in the ancient world, there are very few written histories of the early Roman Republic or its previous monarchy. In fact, historical documentation was not seen on a large scale in the republic until the 3rd century BCE, after the society had already expanded its territories and established itself as one of the great powers of the ancient world. Historians have pieced together a great deal of military history during this time, but there are few references to the culture of the early Roman Republican society. Nevertheless, there are clear movements towards greater government organization, as with the creation of political posts, such as the praetor and the aedile, and the inclusion of the republic's first plebeian leaders.

The republic also held two popular assemblies as part of its governmental system: the Centuriate Assembly and the Tribal Assembly. The Centuriate Assembly was comprised of military leaders and personnel who voted on matters relating to war and peace, electing magistrates who could exercise this military power in various degrees. The Tribal Assembly was comprised of civilians who elected magistrates responsible for passing judgments and making decisions about public legislation.

The Law of the Twelve Tables was the first written document describing the laws of the Roman Republic. Written in 451 BCE, the Twelve Tables were indeed inscribed on twelve bronze tablets that were displayed in the public forum, or marketplace.[9] Upon these tablets were written legal procedures and legislation concerning debts, paternal authority over children, property law, inheritance, and funeral regulations. These documents would form the foundation of all later Roman law doctrine.

Truly, the Roman Republic created one of the first forms of democratic government in the world, and they were exceedingly proud of their system, to the point that they even convinced their conquered enemies of their superiority. Rome became a true colonial empire, building upon its central Italian stronghold with the lands of the Etruscans, Umbri, Samnites, and Celts until nearly all Italy was under its control. In the new lands, Roman consuls erected taxation systems, military conscription, and above all, the idea that to be a

---

[9] "Roman Republic." *Encyclopaedia Britannica*. Web.

part of the Roman Republic was the most glorious privilege in the known world. It was a mindset that rooted itself deeply in member colonies over the following decades and centuries and still holds meaning today.

Chapter Three – 311 BCE

The Seventh Sicilian War

Sicily, a large island located just ten kilometers west of mainland Italy, was the primary theater for a multitude of battles, skirmishes, and regime changes in the first millennium BCE. Positioned at the southwestern reaches of mainland Italy, Sicily was originally colonized by Greeks in the 8th century BCE.[10] Greek cities were mostly built along the eastern and southern sections of the island, with the capital of Syracuse founded in 734 BCE and the city of Messana around the same time.[11]

It was here, in 315 BCE, that the Tyrant of Syracuse, Agathocles, seized the city of Messana, attempting to beat back the encroaching Carthaginians. Four years later, he marched on the remaining Carthaginian cities of Sicily, thus breaking a peace treaty with Carthage and prompting vicious counterattacks.

[10] "Syracuse|Italy." *Encyclopaedia Britannica.* Web.

[11] "Syracuse|Italy." *Encyclopaedia Britannica.* Web.

As the self-proclaimed King of Sicily—since his city was the most populous and powerful of all the Sicilian communities—Agathocles took it upon himself to further impose the will of Greek settlers onto Sicily by pushing back against Carthage and ridding the island of its people. To fortify his own army, Agathocles hired an independent band of mercenaries from Campania, Italy.

It was the Carthaginian Hamilcar Barca, general of that great empire's army, that led the counterattack against the Tyrant of Syracuse. Hamilcar defeated Agathocles at the Battle of the Himera River in 311 BCE, causing the tyrant to retreat to Syracuse while Hamilcar took control over the rest of the island. Triumphant, the Carthaginian general turned on the one remaining Greek city and besieged it.

Agathocles managed to escape the siege and formulated a cunning plan to lead Hamilcar back to Africa. Leading an army of 14,000, the Tyrant of Syracuse marched on the capital city of Carthage. The attack was successful enough: though Agathocles did not capture the city, his army was destructive enough to lure Carthage's primary protector home to defend it. Hamilcar himself, and most of his Sicilian army, returned to Carthage and met the Greeks at the Battle of White Tunis just outside the city.

The Tyrant of Syracuse was astoundingly successful in beating back the returned army with his own troops, but he still could not penetrate the massive fortifications of Carthage itself. Agathocles settled for control of the outlying towns of northern Tunisia before Carthage ousted the Greeks entirely, negotiating a peace treaty with Agathocles whereby he could return to Sicily and maintain control over the eastern half of the island. Carthage retained control over the western half.

Chapter Four - 288 BCE

The Mamertines Take Messana

Following the death of Agathocles in 289 BCE, the tyrant's suspected murderer, Hicetas, took his place.[12] A revolution followed in which Hicetas called for military aid from the Carthaginians, and they gave their support to his claim of leadership in Agathocles' place. At some point after calling in Carthage, Hicetas altogether expelled the Campanian mercenaries hired by his predecessor from Syracuse. Some returned to Campania, but many of them remained in Sicily, in search of a home. Their gaze turned towards the Greek city of Messana.

The mercenaries did not ask to be let in, but rather took Messana by force, killing all the men and forcing the women to act as their wives.[13] They took the places of the dead and integrated themselves inextricably into their new city. Following the slaughter, the mercenaries named themselves the "Mamertines." The name is

---

[12] "Agathocles." *Encyclopaedia Britannica.* Web.

[13] *Warmington, Brian Herbert. Carthage. 1960.*

derived from the word "Mamers," otherwise known as Mars, the war god.[14] The Mamertines stayed in Messana, virtually unchallenged, for two decades.

Hierro II Defeats the Mamertines

After becoming firmly established in Messana, the Mamertines began pillaging the surrounding lands in the northeastern region of Sicily until they encountered the citizens of Syracuse. The new Tyrant of Syracuse, Hierro II, beat the Mamertines back with his army and made it clear that their occupation of Messana was in danger of coming under attack, as well. Determined to hold onto the city they had stolen, the Mamertines sent pleas for help to the two nearest military powerhouses: Rome and Carthage.

Carthage answered the call first, offering to build a Carthaginian garrison at Messana to help with security. They also consulted with Hierro II and gained his promise not to take any further action against the Mamertines. The Mamertines, however, felt that this was not a significant enough effort, and they tried to broker an alliance between Carthage and Rome so that both parties could provide a double layer of protection. The two were not in favor of working together, however. Rome was unsure how to proceed, given that they did not want to lend support to a society that had murdered its way into Messana; Rome was also uncomfortable with the fact that Carthage had so many land holdings in Sicily. After all, Sicily was only a short voyage away from mainland Italy, offering Carthage an easy route by which to lay siege to Rome if it should ever decide to do so.

The matter was put to a vote with the popular assembly in Rome, which decided to grant the Mamertines the support they had asked for. One of the Roman elected consuls, Appius Claudius Caudex, was appointed commander of the military expedition tasked with

---

[14] "Mamertines." *Encyclopaedia Britannica.* Web.

crossing over to Messana. Caudex's first targets were the Syracusan ports since Sicily's hilly, volcanic landscape made it difficult to mount a land attack. The first stages of the military campaign were characterized by skirmishes at sea and port blockades.

Chapter Five – 264 BCE

The Battle of Messana

Immediately prior to the formal outbreak of the first war between Rome and Carthage, there were three main cultural powers in place on Sicily: Carthage in the west, Greek Syracuse in the southeast, and the Mamertines in Messana in the northeast. Hanno led the Carthaginians, Hierro II led Syracuse, the Mamertines worked as a group, and Rome was led by consul Caudex.

Caudex's first act of war was to send a small army to Messana under the leadership of a family member called C. Claudius. Having garnered this wave of military support, the Mamertines forcibly ousted the Carthaginian garrison that had been built within their city as an answer to their own plea for military assistance. They even executed one of the generals of that garrison before he could return to Carthage. The Carthaginian Empire took this news very badly, and immediately the agreement by which Carthage had vowed to help the inhabitants of Messana was voided. Carthage sent its army to Messana not to provide protection but, this time, to attack.

Along the way to the rebel city, Hanno led the Carthaginians to Agrigentum and made an alliance with the people there. Next, the Carthaginians stopped in Sicily to discuss terms with Hierro II, and another powerful ally was made. Together, the allies marched on Messana with the singular goal of destroying the mercenary population within.

In 264 BCE, Caudex led a fresh wave of Roman troops to Sicily, following Claudius, to attack Messana.[15] These troops arrived at the targeted city at approximately the same time as Hanno and Hierro II's armies. Armed with over two Roman legions, Caudex did not engage with his ally's enemies but instead used his own network of allies to ferry the Romans across the waters surrounding the city and into Messana. Though all three leaders were prepared for war, none of them made a move to attack. It seems that all parties were anxious to avoid violence at all costs, perhaps in view of negotiations. After all, despite small-scale fighting, there was not yet open war declared between anyone.

Indeed, the leaders gathered to discuss terms. It was a relatively short period of diplomacy, during which Caudex tried to convince Hierro II to withdraw his troops to Syracuse. The tyrant declined, and no progress was made. The meeting was dismissed, and Hierro II returned to his camp outside the city; Hanno returned to his own, which had not been integrated with that of his allies. The organization of these camps suggests little trust between the allies, which seems reasonable since their only tie was the desired fall of Messana.

Caudex made the first offensive move, attacking the Syracusans. The attack failed to break the enemy camp but caused enough damage to dissuade Hierro II from following up with his campaign. The Syracusans retreated to their city, leaving only Hanno and his Carthaginians to face the Romans and Mamertines. Again, Caudex struck first. Though Hanno could see he stood a chance at fighting off the Romans alone, he soon decided that it wasn't possible for his

---

[15] "First Punic War | Carthage and Rome." *Encyclopaedia Britannica.* Web.

17

single army to defeat both Rome and the Messana guard. Like Hierro II, Hanno turned back and retreated from the outskirts of the city.

Caudex and his legions marched south toward Syracuse, capturing the Carthaginian fort at Echetla but failing to lay successful siege to the powerful city itself. Knowing that his term as Roman consul was due to end soon, the general saw little else to do except head back to Rome. His primary mission—to protect Messana from Carthage—had been successful, though there had been no lasting peace made between any of the belligerents.

Chapter Six – 263 BCE

Rome's Alliance with Syracuse

The Syracusans had named Hierro II king of Syracuse for protecting them from a former military threat. Taking full advantage of his people's gratitude, the former tyrant decided to further elevate his status in their eyes and cement his future role as king. Seeking a political alliance by which to achieve this goal, Hierro married the daughter of Syracuse's esteemed citizen, Leptines.

With Messana's Roman guard back in Italy, Hierro II was temporarily safe from further threats. Because of Syracuse's alliance with Carthage, however, the Romans saw Hierro as a potential enemy whose loyalties to their strong North African neighbor needed to be curbed. In 263 BCE, therefore, Rome gathered an immense army with the intention to march on Hierro II. Its purpose was to either take him into an alliance with Rome or to capture Syracuse.

The expedition had 40,000 men comprised of four Roman legions and a congregation of allied troops.[16] The soldiers marched under

---

[16] Rickard, J. "Roman Alliance with Syracuse." *History of War.* Web. 10 May 2007.

consul Manius Valerius Maximus, elected that same year as one of the co-consuls of the Roman Republic.[17] Maximus landed his army at Messana upon debarking on Sicily since his predecessor's alliance there made it a safe place to set up camp. From there, the Roman legions marched to the south into the territories belonging to Syracuse. Along the way, they seized the Syracusan town of Hadranum and, in doing so, inspired all the other communities to surrender outright. With the path to Syracuse made clear by this preemptive surrender in the hinterland, Maximus easily made his way to the city of King Hierro II.

Within Syracuse, the people were already unhappy about Hierro II's alliance with Carthage. Syracuse had fought Carthage for centuries, and there was a lasting sense of distrust for that nation to the south. Hierro was fully aware of the feelings of his people and, furthermore, did not like his odds against the Roman army as they approached Syracuse. Therefore, he decided to abandon the alliance with Carthage and negotiate a new one with the Romans.

Polybius' account of the beginning of this new alliance was thus: "And when he saw the terror and dismay of the Sicilians, and compared with them the number and crushing strength of the legions of Rome, Hierro began, from a review of all these points, to conclude that the prospects of the Romans were brighter than the prospects of the Carthaginians. Inclining, therefore, from these considerations to the side of the former, he began sending messages to the Consuls, proposing peace and friendship with them."[18]

This time, the alliance lasted for the long term. King Hierro II agreed to pay Rome twenty-five talents up front and subsequently make another fifteen payments to the republic over the course of the fifteen-year treaty. On Rome's part, the republic agreed to formally

---

[17] Barnabas, Crist Bal. *Manius Valerius Maximus Corvinus Messall.* 2012.

[18] Shuckburgh, Evelyn S., Histories of Polybius – Translated from the Text of F. Hultsch. Macmillan and Company, 1889.

recognize Hierro as the king of Syracuse, incorporating the lands within a thirty-mile radius under his regime.

This was the sort of diplomacy that the Roman Republic had been hoping for, and consul Marcus Valerius Maximus' achievements in negotiating a lucrative peace with Syracuse were celebrated in Rome. In addition to the payments from King Hierro II and the avoidance of battle at Syracuse, the Romans now had a secure place to anchor their ships in Sicily. In the coming years of war with Carthage, this saved them an immense amount of travel time and expense.

The Syracusans had just as much to be thankful for. They had avoided the Roman siege of their city and hinterlands and gained the presence of an eternally hungry and needy Roman army. Markets and producers of Syracuse sold goods regularly to the Romans, lining their pockets more than had been possible before the alliance. Farmers around the city grew an abundance of corn and other foods that sustained the armies as generals made strategic decisions about the placement of naval craft and weapons.

Rome looked closely at the signed treaty between their consul and Hierro II and was convinced that there would be no more conflict between the two. Therefore, Rome held off on sending more legions and allowed the Romans already in Sicily to maintain their mutually beneficial status with Hierro and his people.

The Carthaginians, of course, eventually learned of Hierro II's defection from their alliance and were not pleased by the change of circumstances. They did not send warships, however, knowing that Rome already had several legions at Syracuse. Instead, Carthage decided to focus its energy on Agrigentum. There, Carthage gathered its army and took advantage of the city's immense fortifications, making plans for a future assault on Syracuse once the time was right.

Chapter Seven – 262 BCE

The Battle of Agrigentum

After the Romans had acquired the loyalty of Syracuse, the Carthaginians sought to strengthen their forces against the Romans, as they were certain to clash sooner rather than later. In 262 BCE, the Romans attacked Agrigentum to prevent the Carthaginians from using it as a military base to wage war on Rome.[19]

Agrigentum was located near the southern coast of Sicily, where it lay on a plateau encircled by low cliffs and two mountain peaks to the north. A wealthy city, Agrigentum was founded in about 581 BCE by Greeks who traveled there from Gela.[20] Ruled by the tyrant Phalaris from 570 to 554 BCE, the city was famous as the place where Phalaris tortured men to death by roasting them in a brazen bull.[21]

---

[19] Lazenby, John Francis. *The First Punic War: A Military History.* 1996.

[20] "Agrigento." *Encyclopaedia Britannica.* Web.

[21] Ibid.

Agrigentum had a long history as a center of political dispute, having weathered the wars between Athens and Syracuse before beating back the Carthaginians in the 5th century BCE and falling nearly into ruin. Another Greek leader, Timoleon, rejuvenated the city in 338 BCE so that, by the time Rome entered the scene less than a century later, the economy was on the upswing as part of the Carthaginian Empire.[22]

As Carthage and Rome prepared their sides for what seemed like an inevitable conflict, it was Sicily where the bulk of both armies gathered. Expecting war at any moment, the Carthaginian commander of Agrigentum—Hannibal Gisco—gathered the people of nearby farms and villages within the walls of the city. Agrigentum was thought to be an ideal place for protection from other forces. With the Hypsas River on its west side and the Akragas River on its east side, the city had only one way in for an attack, and that generally made for an easily defendable city. This battle led to the first major clash between Carthage and Rome. Both sides knew it was an eventuality, and both had prepared accordingly.

The Roman consuls Lucius Postumius Megellus and Quintus Mamilius Vitulus settled their 40,000 troops into the abandoned fields outside the city and began to lay siege to Agrigentum.[23] As around 50,000 people packed together inside the city, their commander refused to engage the Romans outside the walls. Rome set up its camp a mile away and harvested the people's crops for its own supply, allowing its army to continue the siege unabated.[24] While Gisco hid behind Agrigentum's fortifications, the Romans built double walls around the city to protect themselves from additional Carthaginians attacking them from the hinterlands.

---

[22] Ibid.

[23] Lazenby, John Francis. *The First Punic War: A Military History*. 1996.

[24] Ibid.

Carthage was by no means intent on letting Rome crush its carefully-laid plans, however. While the Romans made plans in Sicily, the Carthaginians had begun building a secondary army of mercenary warriors in Africa. The army was comprised of 50,000 infantry soldiers, 6,000 cavalrymen, and 60 elephants; the mercenaries included Celts, Ligurians, and Iberians.[25] Carthage planned to send this army, under the authority of general Hanno, to Sicily following training. Then, it would set up base in several fortified cities on the island. The army's military generals expected to battle on open ground, under the command of Hannibal Gisco.

The siege went on for five months before the African army finally arrived to fend off the Romans. People inside the city walls were growing desperate by that point, but before a surrender could be extracted from Hannibal, Hanno showed up with troops, cavalry, and war elephants. These long-awaited defenders gave the Agrigentum citizens renewed hope for an end to the siege that didn't involve falling under Roman command. The relief forces not only organized an attack on the Roman forces but also cut off their enemy's supply line.

Rome's alliance with Hierro II of Syracuse was its saving grace. Hierro's own troops broke through the Carthaginian blockade to the Roman camp, restoring the supply line. Rome and Carthage battled for two months before Hanno's army was forced to retreat to the city of Heraclea, the latter's general having lost half of his troops. After seven months of battle, however, Rome's victory was slim. Exhausted and heavily weakened, the Romans were unable to capture Hannibal, who escaped the besieged city and went into hiding.

As Carthage retreated, the Romans allowed their troops to sack Agrigentum and capture its surviving population. The captives, including those of Greek ethnicity who technically had no political

---

[25] Warmington, Brian Herbert. *Carthage*. 1960.

quarrel with Rome at the time, were sold into slavery. Due to this oversight, Sicily's Greek population turned against the Romans. This was a difficult reality for Rome, whose politics, economy, military, and philosophical culture were so heavily—and proudly—based on those of the classical Greeks. Perhaps this explains why consuls Lucius Postumius Megellus and Quintus Mamilius Vitulus were not rewarded for their efforts at Agrigentum, despite having delivered a victory for the Roman Republic.

Following the battle, Rome decided that to succeed fully against Carthage, it must in fact subjugate the whole of Sicily and take power from the northern islands of Sardinia and Corsica as well—as they were outposts for the Carthaginians.

Chapter Eight – 260 BCE

The Battle of the Lipari Islands

The recent success at Agrigentum had left Rome confident in its military prowess, so the republic decided to fortify that territorial strength by building a capable navy. Previously dependent on allies to provide ships and tactical naval strategy, Rome ordered 150 triremes and quinqueremes (battleships powered by lines of rowers) to be built—and their crews trained and drilled—in just two months.[26] Consul Gnaeus Cornelius Scipio took command of the first seventeen ships off the construction line and sailed to Messana. There, he prepared for the upcoming campaign and awaited the rest of the fleet.

On the way, Scipio received a message that the military garrison of Lipari, positioned on a small island to the north of Sicily, was willing to become an ally. Heartened, Scipio made haste to Lipari to cement the deal. As he and his fleet entered the harbor at Lipari, Scipio realized he had been set up to get trapped. There, the Carthaginian fleet was waiting for him, under the authority of Hannibal Gisco. Twenty ships quickly maneuvered to block the Romans from coming into the harbor. Terrified and untested in

---

[26] Goldsworthy, Adrian. *The Fall of Carthage*. 2003.

battle, the Roman ships' crews threw themselves into the water to escape, leaving Scipio to the mercy of his enemies. Gisco took the consul and his brand-new ships captive.

A few days after Scipio was taken captive at Lipari, the remainder of his ships set out, as commanded, for Sicily. Before disembarking there, they met a Carthaginian contingent at the tip of mainland Italy. There were about fifty ships, led by Hannibal. These, however, were unready to encounter the enemy at sea, and Rome's fleet sank half of Hannibal's ships before the general once more managed to escape with the rest of his own fleet. Scipio would not be released for several years.

The Battle of Mylae

Soon afterward, Scipio's co-consul for that year, Gaius Duilius, learned of his colleague's capture and the defeat of that entire brigade. Rome was altogether shocked and embarrassed at Scipio's capture and began referring to him as "Scipio Asina," or "Scipio Ass." Formerly in charge of mainland tactics, Duilius took over the Sicilian campaign, making haste to join the fleet that had just defeated Hannibal's ships.

While the fleet waited in Sicily for their new general to arrive, the crews spent their days manufacturing a variety of naval weapons and new inventions that were expected to give them a crucial edge in battle. One of these inventions was the corvus.[27] Essentially a small bridge that could be raised, lowered, and spun on a central pole at the prow of the Roman ships, the corvus featured a heavy spike on its underside that would pierce the deck of an enemy ship and anchor there, allowing soldiers to walk across its plank and attack in hand-to-hand combat. These machines were completed and ready in the Roman quinqueremes by the time Duilius arrived in Sicily.

---

[27] DeSantis, Marc G. *Rome Siezes the Trident.* 2016.

Having learned that the Carthaginians were raiding Mylae, an island just off the northeastern tip of Sicily, Duilius steered the new Roman fleet in that direction. Upon spotting the enemy warships, the Romans could see that they were outnumbered in terms of ships, but they were confident in their new weapons and pushed on. Hannibal, probably trying to spare as many of his already depleted navy ships from damage as he could, only sent in a few dozen ships to take on Duilius' fleet. These were quickly dispatched. The corvus shocked the Carthaginians, who struggled to free their ships from the boarding plank. The invention was a huge success, and it allowed the Romans to compete in naval battle despite their relatively little knowledge of such tactics.

It was with brute force and prow-to-prow collisions that the Romans took out the enemy ships, bewildering the Carthaginian sailors who were used to more complex maneuvers with their lighter, smaller ships. It makes a great deal of sense that, in tackling naval warfare, Duilius' soldiers—who were more used to land battles as the Romans were—found a way to engage in close combat, as they would have done during a land battle. Though their methods were perhaps less elegant than the tactics of their more experienced enemies, the Romans did manage to win the battle, once more sending Hannibal and what was left of his ships into full retreat.

A series of small-scale battles, many lacking much detail in the histories written by Titus Livius, took place during the following years.

Chapter Nine – 259 BCE

The Battle of Thermae

Meanwhile, in Sicily, the Carthaginian general Hamilcar had assembled his army near the city of Panormus. Upon hearing that the Roman land forces in Sicily were bickering among themselves, Hamilcar decided to capitalize on the situation and take out a large faction of his enemy's army.

Some 6,000 Roman and allied soldiers had separated from the main body of the army and were marching towards Panormus, intent on capturing the city for themselves. Evidently, the argument had been made that Rome should make more offensive attacks, roaming the island and capturing enemy cities at will. The more conservative-minded legionnaires wanted to await specific orders from the consul.

The rift between the two groups caused considerable damage to the collective Roman side because Hamilcar's army located the rebellious faction and crushed them. Nearly the entire wayward army was decimated.

Chapter Ten – 258 BCE

Romans March on Panormus

The Roman consuls elected for the year 258 BCE were Gaius Sulpicius Paterculus and Aulus Atilius Caiatinus (or Calatinus). The two agreed that it was time for Rome to go back on the offensive in Sicily, particularly after the lack of leadership and order they had heard of at Thermae. Their first target was the city of Panormus, where they hoped to lay siege to the fortifications and draw the Carthaginians out into battle.

Panormus refused to play into the hands of the Romans, however, and so the legions moved on, adjusting their strategy to conquer a succession of smaller Sicilian cities. One by one, they attacked and won Hippana, Myttistratum, Enna, and Camarina. Riding this wave of success, the new consuls even went back to the scene of former consul Scipio's humiliation at Lipara. There, they moved in the fleet to blockade the city that had lured in fellow sailors and taken Scipio hostage. Scipio was released around this time, having most likely been ransomed to his countrymen.

Paterculus took the lead in attacking Sardinia after much of Sicily had fallen to Rome's army, foreseeing that the small island to the north could provide the same benefits to Carthage as Sicily. Knowing that the Roman Republic was not safe from Carthage if Italy's peripheral islands were not allied with or conquered by it, plans were made to occupy both Sardinia and Corsica.

Off the coast of the Sardinian city of Sulci, Paterculus' fleet was engaged by Carthage once more—Carthage having developed much the same strategy as Rome's in capturing all nearby islands. Once more, Hannibal Gisco, having escaped at Mylae and taken some time to repopulate his army and his fleet there, led the charge for Carthage. Once prepared, the Carthaginians sailed north to Sardinia and put in port there. To lure the Carthaginians out into the open sea, Rome's fleet made toward the south as if to reach Africa and attack Carthage in Hannibal's absence. The ploy worked, and when Hannibal moved his fleet out of dock at Sulci to pursue, the Romans promptly halted and engaged the enemy. It was a fully naval battle, and though Carthage did not suffer heavy losses, Rome was once again victorious. It had become clear that the Roman Republic was developing into the new naval superpower of the Mediterranean Sea.

Hannibal retreated with his remaining ships to Sulci but abandoned the fleet in the harbor and fled with his men into the city. Despite having potentially saved their lives, Hannibal Gisco faced the wrath of his outraged army, which arrested and crucified him.[28]

---

[28] DeSantis, Marc G. *Rome Siezes the Trident.* 2016.

Chapter Eleven – 257 BCE

The Battle of Tyndaris

While working on ship maintenance onshore north of Sicily, Gaius Atilius Regulus received intelligence that the Carthaginian navy was sailing nearby under the leadership of one Hamilcar, out of striking formation. Being out of formation suggested that the enemy was not preparing to attack, but at any rate, the Romans hurried to put their ships back into the water at Cape Tyndaris.

Panicked, Regulus took the first ten ships that were in the water and set out directly towards the Carthaginians. He hastened to make a defensive attack and was quickly overwhelmed by the enemy fleet. All Roman ships were sunk, except for the one carrying the consul and a full crew. Soon afterward, the rest of the Roman fleet arrived and formed an attack line, corvus machines at the ready. The Romans took down eight Carthaginian ships and captured another ten before Carthage turned around and retreated to the Lipari Islands.[29]

According to historian Polybius, "the land-based armies did nothing worth recording, but occupied themselves with minor and incidental

---

[29] Ibid.

engagements" during this period of the war.[30] Both Rome and Carthage had large and powerful navies by that time, and both were happy to stay off dry land and police their respective territories by sea.

[30] Ibid.

Chapter Twelve – 256 BCE

The Battle of Cape Ecnomus

By the year 256 BCE, the Roman fleet numbered 360 quinqueremes, a number that would have required a full staff of 99,000 rowers.[31] If each ship also carried its maximum capacity of marines on board, the total number of men at sea would have reached nearly 140,000.[32] The sheer magnitude of this naval effort must have required not only Romans from the capital city but also recruits from all of Italy. Historians have posited that to secure such a huge number of rowers and marines, the usual length of an individual's naval service was probably just the summer season.

The main purpose of this unprecedented naval expansion was to launch a campaign directly to Africa, meeting the Carthaginians on their home territory. Certainly, this would have been helpful in extracting enemy forces from the lands surrounding Italy, which had been constantly under pressure for nearly a decade at that point. Furthermore, if Rome's movements toward the south could help flush enough Carthaginians out of Sicily, remaining Republican

---

[31] Ibid.

[32] Ibid.

troops could take advantage of the opportunity to claim large tracts of the island.

The Roman naval units at Messana set sail down the eastern coast of Sicily, around Cape Pachynus (Pachynum/Passero/Passaro), and to Ecnomus to rendezvous with the rest of the fleet. Concerned that the Carthaginians had ramped up their naval fleet and weaponry as well, Rome's fleet traveled in an unorthodox wedge shape, with the two largest ships at the front. Each of these held one of the consuls and led what may have been the largest naval procession in all history.

For his part, Carthage's new general, Hamilcar, knew that the Romans were planning something big and that the upcoming battle would have a serious impact on the future of the war. If Carthage won, the remainder of the war would be confined to Sicily. If Rome won, the fighting would spread into North Africa and potentially wreak havoc on Carthage itself.

The entire Roman fleet was divided into four squadrons, with the first two led by the consuls. These squadrons consisted of the two long sides of the wedge formation. The third squadron consisted of the back edge of the wedge, with the fourth squadron lined up in parallel behind them. The Carthaginians made a simple attacking line, intent on splitting the Roman squadrons into a multitude of small groups and engage in a series of smaller battles.

Carthage planned to encircle the Roman wedge within its line, and to facilitate this, the center of the line held back while the Roman navy approached. The left and right wings of the Carthaginian line plowed ahead, folding around the third and fourth Roman squadrons, while the consuls pressed on, hoping to take advantage of what looked like a sparse central line. It was a dynamic mash-up of offensive formations, but the Romans still had an important edge over their enemies thanks to the corvus. Carthage had no answer to the mechanical boarding anchor, meaning that, in hand-to-hand combat, Rome fared much better.

It was Hamilcar's fleet that was forced to retreat as the consuls gathered up the occupied enemy ships and horse transports. Rome captured a total of sixty-four Carthaginian ships, fifty of which still had their crews on board.[33] Twenty-four Roman ships and thirty of Hamilcar's were sunk, but the overall victory went to Rome. The consuls ordered their fleet ashore for repairs, and when the ships were readied once more, they all set out toward Africa.

---

[33] "Ecnomus, 265 BC." *Livius.org.* 2019.

Chapter Thirteen – 255 BCE

The Siege of Aspis

The fleet was undisturbed for the rest of the voyage, and the Romans first stopped at Cape Hermaeum before landing at Aspis at the northeastern tip of Tunisia. It was here that the Romans chose to start their campaign, some 112 kilometers east of Carthage. Aspis was unready for an attack, though as a Carthaginian-founded city, it was heavily fortified. Rome's first move was to pull its warships onshore; next, the Romans dug a trench around the city and built an enormous palisade around that. The structures ready, Rome began the siege.

This style of city-based warfare was something with which the Romans had plenty of experience. Confidence in their siege tactics, plus the fact that Aspis was largely undefended at the time, meant a clear victory for the Romans. Carthage had not yet moved all its forces back on land, so there was no army on hand that could reach Aspis in time to be of any use. Rome's African campaign was getting off to an excellent start.

Determined to continue the march on Africa, but aware that the war in Sicily and Italy was potentially ongoing, the Romans sent most of their fleet and infantry back to Rome. In North Africa, 15,000 infantrymen, forty ships, and 500 cavalry units remained under the authority of that year's consul, Marcus Regulus.[34] The co-consul, Lucius Manlius Vulso, returned home with the captured Carthaginians on board his ships. This peculiar move left the Romans hugely outnumbered in Africa. However, as the Carthaginians returned from the Mediterranean, they focused their efforts on further fortifying the city of Carthage. Though the opportunity existed for Hasdrubal Barca—son of the late Hanno—to attack the reduced Roman numbers to the east, the order was never given.

Hasdrubal and Bostar were appointed as generals over the Carthaginian army, and while preparations were made to meet the Romans at Carthage, Hamilcar was recalled with his contingent from Sicily. Upon his return home, Hamilcar brought 5,000 infantrymen and 500 cavalrymen.[35]

The Battle of Adis

From the conquered city of Aspis, the Romans moved westward into inland Tunisia. They made camp while awaiting orders to attack the enemy's capital city, but Regulus was not idle during that time. He moved about the countryside with his army and made various attacks on smaller cities, plundering what he liked and facing little resistance. The Carthaginians kept a distant watch on the movement of the Romans and soon spotted them on the outskirts of the city of Adis.

Carthage had more cavalry and elephants at that point, but the generals were hesitant to enter into battle. Even as Regulus ordered his men to lay siege to Adis, Carthage held back at first— probably since their camp was located on a rocky ridge that would be very difficult to traverse quickly while marching in to break the siege.

---

[34] "Siege of Aspis." *History of War*. Web.

[35] DeSantis, Marc. *Rome Seizes the Trident*. 2016.

Eventually, Carthage sent in its mercenary army to face off with the Romans, which was ultimately unsuccessful. The Carthaginian camp was captured; however, the elephants and cavalry escaped back to the capital.

The Battle of Tunis

Carthage was clearly struggling to repel the Romans, both at sea and on land, and at one point during this period, its leaders attempted negotiations with Rome to stop the endless siege warfare and naval attacks. The Romans, however, wanted a great deal of money in exchange for their peace, and Carthage couldn't agree to the terms. So, the war continued, and Carthage looked for ways to improve its performance in battle.

The answer lay with a group of Greek mercenaries whose training and experience in Hellenistic-style warfare was second to none. The Greeks were famous for their ability to organize and manage vast armies, and when one loudmouthed Spartan by the name of Xanthippus was made a military advisor, he did great justice to that reputation. Xanthippus was very vocal about his disapproval of the Carthaginian commanders, and thus, over the winter of 255 BCE, he was given free rein to whip the Punic army into fighting shape.[36] The army swelled to 12,000 infantrymen, 4,000 cavalrymen, and 100 war elephants.[37]

The Roman army at that time was based in the city of Tunis, near the Bagradas River. With Regulus still in charge, troops were extremely confident in their abilities and perhaps unaware of the major changes that had been made to the enemy army. Their formation of choice was infantry at the center and cavalry on both wings. Xanthippus had taught the Carthaginians to use the phalanx formation—a dense square of infantry soldiers armed with spears—with the Greek

---

[36] "Battle of Tunis, 255 BC." *History of War.* Web.

[37] "Battle of Tunis, 255 BC." *History of War.* Web.

mercenaries on the right, behind a line of elephants, and the cavalry split between both wings.

It was the Carthaginians who advanced on the Roman legions this time, beginning the battle with an elephant attack directed at the enemy infantry. The cavalries on the flanks faced off, but with Rome's horses outnumbered four to one, Carthage made quick work of its opponents. Rome's infantry succeeded on one end, pushing back the mercenaries who fled to their camp. The elephants did their job well, essentially blocking the Romans from reaching the phalanx to take it apart, which left the Roman infantry vulnerable to a double-sided attack from the Carthaginian cavalry. Having gained the upper hand, Carthage slaughtered every Roman left on the field, except 2,000 soldiers who had caused the retreat of the mercenary block.[38] These had to be rescued by the fleet, while Regulus was captured and taken prisoner.

It was the first significant victory for Carthage and one that neither side would easily forget.

---

[38] Ibid.

Chapter Fourteen – 251 BCE

The Battle of Panormus

With the Romans entirely flushed out of Africa, the theatre of war reverted to Sicily. It was in 251 BCE, near the end of the year, that the Carthaginian general Hasdrubal believed he had the opportunity to regain the upper hand in Sicily. He knew that the Roman Republic elected two new consuls each year and that there was always a changeover period during which the old consuls left Sicily and the new ones embarked from Rome. This particular year, an ex-consul left Sicily early, leaving consul Caecilius Metellus at Panormus with a small retinue.

Hasdrubal advanced from Lilybaeum with the main Carthaginian army, moving towards Panormus confidently. The troops stopped at the hinterlands of the city to regroup and draw up a battle plan, at which point Caecilius was forced to make his own defensive plans for the city Rome had held for eight years. The consul landed on a plan to lure Hasdrubal into a trap outside the walls of Panormus, whereby he could use the fortifications of Panormus against Hasdrubal. The city was already behind strong walls, and the ditch dug by Rome during the siege remained. A river ran its course between the city and the Carthaginian army, so Caecilius waited for

Hasdrubal's troops to enter the water before setting a line of Roman troops upon them. A second line was placed in front of the trench.

The city was indeed well protected, but Hasdrubal had a troupe of war elephants that attacked both lines of Romans, and these pushed the consul's men back into their own ditch. Caecilius, however, had expected this very thing; with the Roman troop lines out of the way, the soldiers positioned in the walls and towers could aim their spears down at the elephants. Troops in the ditch joined in the barrage, panicking the elephants and driving them away through the Carthaginian lines.

Consul Caecilius' trap had worked perfectly. With the bulk of the elephants gone, he unleashed a horde of troops through a gate upon Hasdrubal's left wing and soon crippled the attacking army. It was a massive defeat for Carthage, and Hasdrubal's army was almost completely decimated. Roman legions captured sixty elephants, many of which were sent to Rome.[39] Panormus remained in Roman control.

---

[39] "Battle of Panormus." *History of War*. Web.

Chapter Fifteen – 250 BCE

The Siege of Lilybaeum

With one major Carthaginian stronghold left, which was the city of Lilybaeum, the Romans launched a fleet of 200 ships to Sicily under the command of both consuls, Gaius Atilius Regulus—son of the captured former consul—and Lucius Manlius Vulso.[40] Of Lilybaeum, Polybius said, "Its capture would facilitate [the Romans] taking the war to Libya."[41] On the other hand, if Rome failed at this campaign, it faced a major setback that could put off its plans to conquer North Africa for good.

Regulus and Vulso got to work in the usual way, splitting their army in half and putting one on each side of Lilybaeum. Troops dug a trench around the fortified city and built palisades along the trench so that the city was completely cut off from outside help or supplies.

While the trenches and fences were still under construction, Rome began small-scale attacks on the fortifications, specifically upon its defensive towers. Through painstaking attacks, the Romans pulled

---

[40] "Battle of Tunis, 255 BC." *History of War*. Web.

[41] Hall, Joshua R. "The Siege of Lilybaeum." *Ancient World Magazine*. 2018.

down seven towers, but the remaining ones proved more difficult to take apart. They brought in rams and other devices to hack away at the supports, possibly even using catapults to hammer boulders at the sides of the towers.

Inside the city were 10,000 Carthaginian troops under the command of Himilco.[42] Himilco did not stay hidden behind the safety of the city's walls, however, but ordered his troops to build an extra layer of walls within the outer fortifications and to actively target the enemy soldiers in charge of pulling down the towers. The Carthaginians launched many attacks against the siege machines, aiming to set the catapults, rams, and other engines aflame. Their efforts were somewhat productive, but they were unable to put a stop to the siege altogether.

Unsure of how long they could hold out, the Carthaginians grew anxious inside the walls of Lilybaeum, and some officers from mercenary units decided that their best course of action was to surrender. Without consulting with Himilco or the allied troops, these officers exited the city walls and requested to meet with Roman officials. Apparently, these defectors believed that if they could make an agreement with the Romans, their fellows still within the walls of the fortress city would thank them for having taken such bold action.

There was a man within the Carthaginian ranks, however, who discovered the plan of these mercenaries and reported it to Himilco. The man was a Greek mercenary himself, and he had performed a similar duty years earlier when a group of Syracusan soldiers planned to abandon their allies at the besieged city of Akragas. Himilco knew that he needed to hold his defensive army together if he hoped to protect the city, so he met with the remaining mercenary leaders and offered them extra money to stay with him and the Carthaginians. The monetary motivation worked, and the remaining

---

[42] Hall, Joshua R. "The Siege of Lilybaeum." *Ancient World Magazine.* 2018.

mercenaries pledged ongoing loyalty to Himilco and the cause of Lilybaeum.

The city's defenders pressed on, struggling against the Roman siege works until, one night, the weather changed, bringing heavy winds that blew in the direction of the siege machines. Some of the Greek mercenaries were inspired by this, believing that they could use the wind in their favor and set all the Roman's machines on fire at once, effectively wiping out the entire arsenal. They brought their idea to Himilco, who agreed it was an excellent course of action, and they prepared to strike at an appointed time. When the time came, the Greeks flooded out of the city with torches, setting light to anything that would take the flame. Since the siege engines had been in use for long months, the wood was dry and cracked and made for ideal kindling.

The strong winds helped the flames along, spreading fire from machine to machine and causing chaos within the Roman ranks. Embers took to the air and sparked further fires until the siege line was thick with smoke and flame, and when the Romans tried to put out the fires, they were met with a hail of Carthaginian spears. When the flames finally died down, the Romans found themselves without any engines with which to continue the assault of Lilybaeum; it was a clear victory for the Carthaginians, once again thanks to the ingenuity and skill of their Greek mercenaries.

Chapter Sixteen – 249-241 BCE

The Siege of Drepana

The Siege of Drepana took place between 249 and 241 BCE. Drepana was a naval port in western Sicily that the Romans saw as a worthwhile target. Rome had not been a particularly strong naval force up until now. They'd always relied on their strong legions of men to secure most of their battles, and naval prowess was yet to be mastered.

Drepana was to highlight this fact. The battle was a foray into an un-mastered type of warfare for the Romans and a sign that they had much work to do if they wished to achieve naval superiority and avoid such losses as they saw at Drepana. Under Pulcher, at least 39,000 men in the Roman army were lost, either to death or capture by the Carthaginians. Only a scant few Romans escaped death or capture by reaching the shoreline and escaping on land. Ninety-three Roman ships were lost, and Pulcher was blamed and heavily ostracized when he returned to Rome. He was tried and pronounced guilty at court, and then large fines were levied against him. He nearly paid with his life, as execution was considered.

Pulcher's opponent at Drepana was Adherbal. He was a skilled naval warrior, and that, paired with the miscalculations of Pulcher, sealed the fate of the Romans. When Pulcher's ships sailed too close to the shore, Adherbal moved his ships out of the harbor and trapped the Roman ships inside. He made a spectacle of the captured Roman ships and a huge number of captives, and he was hailed a Carthaginian hero. This terrible experience in naval warfare hit the Romans so hard that they did not rebuild a proper naval force for seven years.

This naval battle of the First Punic War highlighted the importance of a strong naval force for the Romans while giving the Carthaginians cause to hope that they may indeed overcome the strength of the Romans. Holding on to Drepana was very important to the Carthaginians, as it allowed them to continue to support their other ports being besieged by Rome. They could access and supply these ports from the sea rather than breaking through Roman legions on land, which would be much harder for them. For this same reason, Rome too would have liked to capture Drepana.

The Battle of Phintias

In 249 BCE, in the First Punic War, the Carthaginian fleets under Carthalo were pitted against the Roman Republic under Lucius Junius Pullus. The events of this battle were written a little differently by Polybius and Diodorus later, but the results of the battle remain the same.[43][44]

The Roman fleet was intercepted by the Carthaginians off Phintias, so it sought shelter rather than move any further toward Carthalo and his ships. Bad weather was coming in, and Carthalo had his ships move off to the east to take refuge from the storms, but Pullus did not take the weather warnings to heart or make any protective maneuvers against it. As recorded by Polybius, "When the weather now became stormy, and they were threatened with a heavy gale

---

[43] Diodorus Siculus. *Library of History*. Translated by Francis Walton. 1957

[44] Polybius. *The Histories*. Translated by W. R. Paton. 1922

from the open sea, the Carthaginian captains who were acquainted with the locality and with the weather signs, and foresaw and prophesied what was about to happen, persuaded Carthalo to escape the tempest by rounding Cape Pachynus. He very wisely consented, and with great labor, they just managed to get around the cape and anchor in a safe position."[45] Diodorus writes that the survivors of the storm made their way to Lilybaeum with the last two ships that survived the storm.

This failure to heed the weather, in the end, cost the Romans all but two of their ships to the storm. What was left in ruins was raided by the Carthaginians, and the Romans again delayed any further naval efforts until 242 BCE.

Lucius Junius was captured by Carthalo's forces at some point and then released, but when he returned to Rome, he committed suicide because of his failure at Phintias.

The Naval Battle of Aegates

The Carthaginian and Roman fleets met on March 10, 241 BCE, in the Battle of the Aegates.[46] This naval battle saw Hanno in command of the Carthaginians and Catulus overseeing the Romans, with Falto in charge during the battle. This was to be the last battle of the First Punic War, which lasted twenty-three years.

Carthage's army was blocked in by the Romans but still held Sicily. The Romans sought to increase their blockade to the sea, but the Carthaginians had more ships. As they tried to move supplies into

---

[45] Polybius. *The Histories.* Translated by W. R. Paton. 1922

[46] Holmes, R. *Battlefield: Decisive Conflicts in History.* Oxford University Press. 2006.

Sicily, the Romans intercepted them. At this point, the Roman's naval forces had better training, and in this sea battle, they overturned the Carthaginians, ending the battle and the war in favor of the Romans.

Because of this defeat, Carthage finally agreed to a treaty for peace with the Romans, and the Treaty of Lutatius, negotiated between Catulus and Hamilcar Barca, was signed. In it, the Carthaginians agreed to leave Sicily and promised not to attack Syracuse. They were to release their prisoners of war and pay war reparations.

The treaty was later altered somewhat before being adopted, but in the end, Carthage was given just ten years in which to pay the reparations of 3,200 talents and had to leave not only Sicily but also the islands of Ustica and the Aegadian Islands off the coast of Sicily.

Rome had succeeded in becoming one of the most powerful armies in all the Mediterranean.

Chapter Seventeen – 240-237 BCE

The Mercenary War

The problem for Carthage following the treaty with Rome was that the empire now had to take responsibility for a huge number of mercenary soldiers who still flooded Sicily. By Rome's stipulations, the army was to be disbanded, and this meant a sudden influx of tens of thousands of mercenaries into Carthage. They wanted to be paid for their services, and it was clear that if they weren't compensated in a timely manner, Carthage could potentially face the wrath of its own hired soldiers.

To avoid conflict with the mercenaries, Carthage arranged to bring them back to Carthage in small groups that could be managed. These groups were too small to pose any real threat to the empire, so if each could be paid and made to leave the city before the next group of incoming mercenaries arrived from Sicily, order was kept. Trouble started, however, when payments could not be made, and groups of paid mercenaries lingered in the city, causing trouble on the streets. Finally, city officials had to request that the mercenaries leave for the city of Sicca Veneria with their families to await payment.

Though the movement of mercenaries into Sicca Veneria saved Carthage from violence, the displaced warriors still proved dangerous. While awaiting their overdue payments, the mercenaries started to make demands for late payment interest, which of course, the empire could never afford. The first round of negotiations led nowhere, so for the second round, Carthage pulled Hanno the Great out of the discussions due to the mercenaries' distrust of him. In his stead was placed a man named Gresco. Still, the talks broke down, and Gresco was taken hostage by the mercenaries. Thus began the Mercenary War.

The rogue mercenary army was not alone in its fight against Carthage, either, since the neighboring Libyans had been heavily taxed of their crops during the First Punic War. Eager for retribution, Libya sent 70,000 men to aid in the war against Carthage.[47] The overall result was a decisive victory for Carthage, despite the numerous allied foes set against them, and General Hamilcar Barca made his first appearance as a despotic and desperate war leader. After the Battle of the Saw, Barca ordered the remaining 45,000 mercenaries to be slaughtered—Carthage would have no debts to the hired soldiers, nor would it risk any remaining enemies. [48]

The Mercenary War lasted from 240-237 BCE, and when it was finished, Carthage felt considerably relieved—as well as confident in its power. The empire wasted no time after crushing the Libyans and the rebel army in announcing to the Roman Republic that it was claiming sovereignty over Sardinia. Sardinia had been conquered by Rome while Carthage was busy fighting the Mercenary War, and Rome had no intention of handing it over to anyone. Furthermore, as if to cement this point, Rome promptly annexed Corsica as well, completing the occupation and control of all three large islands off the west coast of Italy.

---

[47] "The Outbreak of the Second Punic War." *Sites at Penn State.* Web. 2020.

[48] "The Outbreak of the Second Punic War." *Sites at Penn State.* Web. 2020.

The Carthaginian Leaders

Carthage had no royal family, but it did have a respected line of military generals who were significantly important during the Punic Wars. Hannibal Barca was born in 247 BCE to Hamilcar Barca, the latter a significant character in the wars.[49] Following the heavy losses of the Carthaginians following the First Punic War, young Hannibal would have seen his nation's lands stripped away by the Romans. For safety, the elder Barca took his son to Iberia. They left in 237, when Hannibal was ten years old.[50]

Hamilcar continued to add new territories to the Carthaginian empire from his base in Iberia, replacing those that had been taken away by the Romans. Hannibal observed his father's obsession as he grew into a young man, taking on part of it himself. Father and son lived in a world that was ultimately defined by the feud between the Romans and the Carthaginians, and this feeling was mirrored in every part of the Barca family.

---

[49] "Hannibal Barca." *Livius.org.* Web.

[50] Ibid.

Chapter Eighteen – 229-226 BCE

When Hamilcar died in 229 BCE, his son-in-law Hasdrubal the Fair took over the governorship of Iberia and took charge of Hamilcar's armies.[51]

Whereas his father-in-law had used the military, Hasdrubal attempted diplomacy, and it paid off. As had always been the case between warring empires, intermarriage played an important role in the cooling of tempers. Hannibal Barca married a native Iberian princess by the name of Imilce, deftly entwining her culture with his own, both of which stood firmly independent of Roman rule. It is believed that Hannibal even traveled to Carthage while Hasdrubal governed Spain, visiting the city of his birth and drawing his own conclusions as to his future role in that part of the world.

A great politician, Hasdrubal the Fair was by no means content to accept Carthaginian landholders as they were. He established a new Iberian capital in about 227 BCE, called New Carthage.[52] The new capital was located on a peninsula with two working harbors, making it an ideal base from which to direct military campaigns

---

[51] Ibid.

[52] Ibid.

throughout Iberia. The Romans frequently sent their own troops there to prevent further losses, but they often found it easier to negotiate with the savvy warlord. Before a deal was struck, Hasdrubal had conquered Hemeroscopium, Alonis, and Alicante, all Greek colonies of Massilia, an ally of Rome. In 226 BCE, the Romans convinced Hasdrubal to leave the remaining Massilian colonies alone. In exchange, he was permitted to rule over the cities he'd already captured.[53]

Though Hasdrubal made these negotiations independently of the Carthaginian government, he neither pushed for his own independent nation nor called himself a king. It was a time of intense fragmentation for the Carthaginian empire, and such independent behavior was probably only tolerated because there was little else the government of Carthage could do. It hoped that Hasdrubal was ultimately acting for the benefit of Carthage, and indeed it seems he was.

---

[53] "Hasdrubal the Fair." *Livius.org*. Web.

Chapter Nineteen – 225-219 BCE

Diplomacy Between the Wars

In the year 225 BCE, Rome's foremost enemies were the Celts, also known as the Gauls, who lived mostly in the western and middle parts of the continent. Rome, having already conquered the Gallic region of Cisalpine Gaul in northern Italy, was growing ever more confident in its military prowess and therefore set its target on the alliance of Gauls migrating into Italy.

There were further campaigns against the Celts that were not just based on military might: political maneuvers were designed to further oppress the remaining Celtic populations in Roman territory, such as the 232 BCE law allocating large pieces of formerly Celtic land to poor Romans settlers.[54] Subsequently, members of the Celtic Boii and Insubres tribes paid mercenaries from Transalpine Gaul to join them and fight against Rome. Alarmed at the alliance, Rome responded by mobilizing troops from Hispania.

Moving the legions from Hispania back to Italy to prepare for war meant leaving the region open to Gallic or Carthaginian control. Unwilling to let the Celtic issue go unheeded, however, Rome

---

[54] Mineo, Bernard. *A Companion to Livius.* 2014.

decided to partner with the Carthaginian Empire and cover more area. Specifically, Carthaginian general Hasdrubal the Fair was granted full control of Hispania while the Romans were away.[55]

Ultimately, the Romans, under the authority of consuls Gaius Atilius Regulus and Lucius Aemilius Papus, defeated the Celtic alliance and thereby gained further influence in northern Italy.

In 221 BCE, Hasdrubal the Fair was killed by a Celtic mercenary in the city he had founded, New Carthage.[56] Hannibal Barca succeeded him as ruler of the conquered Iberian lands and foremost general of the Carthaginian armies. At twenty-six years of age, he was duly elected by the government. Hannibal Barca favored his father's aggressive military tactics over his predecessor's slightly more diplomatic approach, and his behavior makes it clear that Hannibal held a deep-seated grudge against the Romans. He attacked native groups within Spain, going against the treaty Hasdrubal had carefully drafted with Rome.

In 220 BCE, Hannibal's army captured Salamanca, followed the next year by Saguntum, a Roman ally.[57] To Hannibal's benefit, Rome's own armies were busy fighting yet another enemy in the Second Illyrian War. Thus occupied, Rome was unable to send reinforcement to Saguntum, which subsequently fell to Hannibal. Even then, it was unclear to members of both parties whether the occupation of Saguntum by Hannibal was legally considered grounds for retribution for breaking the treaty since neither Carthage nor Hannibal had signed the document. Nevertheless, Rome was angry at the attack and demanded that the Carthaginian government punish Hannibal.

---

[55]

[56] Ibid.

[57] "Hannibal Barca." *Livius.org*. Web.

The government considered its options but took its time in making any confident conclusions. While the government members argued amongst themselves, Hannibal continued his military campaign to expand Carthage's territory. His brother Hasdrubal—not to be confused with the previous governor—was placed in command of Iberia.

Chapter Twenty – 218 BCE

Under the terms of surrender in 241 BCE, Carthage, up to that point having lost the longest war in ancient history, agreed to withdraw from Sicily and pay reparations to Rome. The First Punic War was tremendously expensive to both sides, but the seemingly inexhaustible wealth of Rome—as well as its growing network of allies—kept the republic afloat in the years following the peace treaty with Carthage.

As the new rulers of the oceans, the Romans took over the Carthaginian mantle. If Carthage were to wrest control back from its arch-enemy, it would have to fight on land, which would be an expensive endeavor. No such undertaking was seriously considered or carried out for at least a decade. That did not mean, however, that either the Romans or the Carthaginians hesitated in waging war on other enemies throughout the Mediterranean.

Hamilcar Barca was recalled from Sicily at the end of the war and joined in the military campaign of Hanno the Great, who had recently made major conquests in Libya. While Carthage was distracted, Rome took control of Sardinia. It was a heavy blow to the

Carthaginians, who had come to rely on regular shipments of grain from that island.

The Carthaginians had to look elsewhere for a source of money to finance their armies in Libya without a large fleet, and having lost their strategically important fortresses in Sicily, Corsica, and Sardinia. They found the answer in Hispania, where they had connections to old Phoenician colonies and a rich supply of silver that had already been established. Accordingly, in 237 BCE, Hamilcar Barca was dispatched to extend the boundaries of Carthaginian territory throughout Hispania.

Hamilcar achieved his goal, establishing a base at Gades and founding the new city of Acra Leuce.[58] Continually campaigning and offering alliances with local tribes and cities, he gained local recruits and amassed a 50,000-strong army with 100 elephants.[59] Tribute was taken from each conquered city, either in the form of fighting men or money.

Hamilcar Barca drowned during battle at the Judar River in 229 BCE, meaning that Hasdrubal took command of the armies.[60] He added 10,000 infantrymen and 8,000 cavalry soldiers to the military, doubling the number of war elephants in his service to 200.[61]

The Battle of Ebro River

Hannibal pointedly crossed the river Ebro in 218 BCE, thereby pressing onward past the boundary with Rome promised by Hasdrubal the Fair.[62] He intended to complete the conquest of Iberia,

---

[58] Ibid.

[59] Ibid.

[60] "Hamilcar Barca." *Encyclopaedia Britannica*. Web.

[61] Ibid.

[62] Ibid.

taking away Rome's remaining holdings there, as well as conquering its remaining allies.

When the Roman Republic realized what was happening, they stopped diplomatic outreach with the Carthaginian government and mobilized their troops once more. Sending soldiers flooding once more into Sicily, Rome declared war, beginning the Second Punic War.

Scipio thought it best to launch a naval battle against the Carthaginians at this point, and he obtained twenty ships for his fleet from allies in the Greek city of Massilia.

When the Carthaginian fleet under Hasdrubal arrived at the Ebro River and anchored, they disembarked their ships to forage for supplies. Hasdrubal posted scouts to watch for Roman activity during this time, but there were no ships out to watch for Scipio's fleet. Two Massalian vessels saw the anchored ships and sailed to find the Romans, who were near Tarraco, and make them aware of the Carthaginians' location. The Romans were a mere ten miles north of the Carthaginians who had anchored and were foraging.

Scipio's Roman fleet immediately set sail toward the anchored ships. Hasdrubal's scouts saw the Romans approach and sent out fire signals to warn the Carthaginians, who were forced to hurriedly take to their ships and sail out in a jumbled manner. The Romans had managed to surprise the Carthaginian fleet quite effectively and also outnumbered their force by more than ten ships. The Romans sank four of the Carthaginian ships and captured two. Many crews abandoned their ships on the beaches and fled.

Hasdrubal marched back to Carthage after this battle rather than risk more attacks from the water and dismissed the Iberian crews that had performed badly in the sea battle. This caused the rebellion in the Turdetani tribe, which Hasdrubal would then be occupied in managing. Carthage sent him 4,000 infantrymen, as well as 500 cavalry soldiers, to deal with the rebellion before he once again went up against the Romans in 215.

The Battle of Lilybaeum

The first naval battle of the Second Punic War was at Lilybaeum. The Carthaginians had raided the Lipari Islands in 218 BCE with twenty quinqueremes (warships), and eight more had attacked Vulcano island. When the Syracuse navy captured three of the ships that had been blown into the Straits of Messina by a storm, they learned from the crews that the Carthaginians were planning to attack Lilybaeum. Hiero II, who was at Messina, warned the Romans under Marcus Aemilius Lepidus, and so they met the Carthaginians. The Romans had put together legions on their ships and filled up on provisions for a lengthy time at sea. Lepidus also put sentinels on the coast to lessen the chance of being surprised when the Carthaginian ships did arrive.

The Carthaginians planned to sail at night and arrive at Lilybaeum at dawn. The Romans, of course, were not surprised, as their lookouts had seen them early on. The Romans were outnumbered, but— because they had so many men on each ship—when they did get close to their enemy's ships, they could board and capture them. The ships that hadn't been captured retreated and could not establish a base in Sicily.

The Battle of Rhone Crossing

In 218 BCE, the Carthaginian army under Hannibal Barca met the Volcae tribe in the Battle of Rhone Crossing.[63] The Volcae tribe was made up of Gauls working for the Roman army, which was camped near Massalia. They hoped to stop the Carthaginians before they crossed the river and invaded Italy. The Carthaginians under Hanno sent troops farther up the river to cross and get behind the Gauls. Hannibal Barca took troops across the river once Hanno signaled that his men were in place. When the Gauls moved on Hannibal,

---

[63] Bagnall, N. *The Punic Wars: Rome, Carthage and the Struggle for the Meditteranean.* Random House. 2008.

Hanno's forces took them from behind. Hence, the Carthaginians successfully crossed the Rhone River the same day as the battle took place. The next day Hannibal moved some of his elephants on rafts, while some swam.

The Carthaginian army regrouped on the eastern bank of the river, and Hannibal headed toward the Alps by traveling along the river. When Scipio and his Roman army found the emptied camp of the Carthaginians, he sent his army to sail to Iberia while he returned to Italy to deal with the approaching Hannibal.

Hannibal Crosses the Alps

With Rome victorious at the end of the First Punic War, the Roman Republic had become the foremost naval power in the Mediterranean. Carthage, eager to regain political and economic power, had campaigned to colonize Iberia, the region of islands and coastal territories to the west of Italy. There, the Carthaginians found various tribes living among mineral-rich landscapes they desperately wanted to bring under their own authority.

General Hamilcar Barca headed the colonization missions, and in 218 BCE, Hamilcar's son Hannibal was in command of the Carthaginian forces in Iberia.[64] Under Hannibal's leadership, the resources of Iberia were collected and sold, the funds used to amass a larger army than before. Though the enlarged army was meant for Italy, it got its first taste of battle at the city of Saguntum in Iberia. Sagantum was allied with the Roman Republic, but far from Rome and surrounded by Carthaginian outposts, it had little protection from Hannibal's forces.

The attack of Sagantum informally marked the beginning of the Second Punic War.

---

[64] Pillalamarri, Akhilesh. "Hannibal Vs. Rome." *The National Interest.* Web.

Once the Carthaginians enjoyed victory over the Roman army in Hispania, Hannibal decided it was necessary to make the next move on the enemy within Italy itself. To meet the Romans on their home ground, Hannibal and his army embarked on a five-month, thousand-mile journey from Hispania to the plains of Italy in 218 BCE.[65] Along the way, they crossed the Pyrenees, the Languedoc, the Rhone, and the Alps, with an estimated 38,000 infantrymen and 8,000 cavalrymen.[66] Unwilling to go into battle without his biggest assets, Hannibal brought thirty-seven African war elephants along with the troops.[67] It was an undertaking completely without precedent and one that would be remembered for more than 2,000 years.

No Carthaginian accounts of the journey still exist, making the closest contemporary documentation those of the Greek historian Polybius (written seventy years later) and Roman historian Livius (nearly two centuries later). Both historians referenced the journals of a Carthaginian soldier, though this book does not exist anymore. Because of this lack of primary sources, the exact route Hannibal's army took from Spain to Rome is unknown. Much fuss has been made over dozens of theories, but there remains no convincing proof of one route over another. Suffice it to say that the route was long and treacherous.

The Alps, which stretch 1,200 kilometers east to west across the northern border of Italy, had provided adequate protection from conquering enemies for thousands of years until Hannibal boldly dared to cross them. Some of the route has been made clear by Livius and Polybus, who documented the beginning of the

---

[65] Ball, Philip. "The truth about Hannibal's route across the Alps." *Guardian*. Web. 2016.

[66] Ibid.

[67] Lidz, Franz. "How and where did Hannibal cross the Alps?" *Smithsonian Magazine*. 2017.

Carthaginian army's ascent of the Alps from the Rhône Valley in Gaul. Though the land was rocky and unfriendly to the foreigners, it was not uninhabited. Mountain tribes living along the route attacked some of Hannibal's party, dropping boulders and setting ambushes, as it made its way eastward.

Tribespeople thinned out by the time the army began its descent into Italy, but the mountains themselves were rockier, steeper, and more dangerous on the way down. Furthermore, the paths used by the Carthaginians were narrower than before. Polybius wrote:

"Because of the snow and of the dangers of his route [Hannibal] lost nearly as many men as he had done on the ascent. Since neither the men nor the animals could be sure of their footing because of the snow, any who stepped wide of the path or stumbled, overbalanced and fell down the precipices. The track was too narrow for the elephants or even the pack animals to pass. At this point, the soldiers once more lost their nerve and came close to despair."[68]

Livius describes the path as the following:

"A narrow cliff falling away so sheer that even a light-armed soldier could hardly have got down it by feeling his way and clinging to such bushes and stumps as presented themselves."[69]

The general tried to find a different path by which his army could descend, but the options were either too steep or too slippery with mud and snow. With nowhere else to go, Hannibal told his troops that if they needed a road, they would have to build it. The soldiers set to work building a road from the rock and rubble of the mountain itself, which eventually served to get men, horses, and mules down below the snow line.

---

[68] Ball, Philip. "The truth about Hannibal's route across the Alps." *Guardian.* Web. 2016.

[69] Livius. "Hannibal in the Alps."

The elephants, however, could not follow. To move the war elephants down the slope, Hannibal's army spent three days widening the road. Every day of the build, the animals grew thirstier, hungrier, and more desolate. Both Polybius and Livius wrote that the original impasse Hannibal met at this point in the journey was caused by fallen rocks. According to Polybius, there was new rockfall over an older landslide. Researchers every century since the momentous expedition have tried to find evidence for the exact route the Carthaginian general took along the Alps, and in 2004, geomorphologist Bill Mahaney of York University in Toronto found strong evidence for that very place along the Col de Traversette path. The Col de Traversette sits at an altitude of 10,000 feet, marking the border between modern Italy and France.[70] There is an old track of rubble leading out of the path, which is believed by some to be remnants of Hannibal's own engineered road.

Researchers suspect that it was not Hannibal's original intent to come down this particular path, given the increased risk from rockfall, narrow passages, and slippery, steep sections. It may be that if he did indeed choose this route, he did so to avoid the Gauls who lived along the mountain's easier passes. Gallic tribes were numerous throughout this region, and various kings and leaders made for vicious enemies. At the sight of a huge convoy through their territory— complete with supplies, weaponry, and horses—any reasonable Gaul's thoughts would turn to plunder.

At a peat bog, not much further down the mountain from the Col de la Traversette, researchers have found what may be further evidence of Hannibal's crossing. In this case, it comes in the form of fine-grained soil at a depth of thirty centimeters—suggesting that around 218 BCE, this area came under some extremely heavy foot traffic.[71] Furthermore, the mud at that level contains DNA found in clostridia

---

[70] Cook, Stephen. "Hannibal Lecture." *Guardian*. 1999.

[71] Ball, Philip. "The truth about Hannibal's route across the Alps." *Guardian*. Web. 2016.

bacteria, which is commonly present in horse and human intestines. They've even located what seems to be a tapeworm egg from a type of the parasite that grows in horses.

Whether the Carthaginian army passed along the Col de la Traversette and the nearby bog or not, they did make their way into Italy after three days of marching down from their newly-built road. Once in the northern Italian plains, Hannibal gave everyone time to rest, eat, and restore their health before moving south to face Rome head-on.

The Battle of Cissa

With his troops adequately rested, it was the summer of 218 BCE when Hannibal eventually set out for the plains of central Italy with tens of thousands of infantry and cavalry behind him. They marched into Gaul, intent for Italy, leaving the newly-conquered territories above the Ebro River in the hands of a contingent guard.

Roman general Gnaeus Cornelius Scipio Calvus sailed to Iberia with 20,000 infantrymen, 2,200 cavalrymen, and sixty quinqueremes to meet the Carthaginian threat there.[72] He was welcomed by the Greek cities he stopped at along the way and completely surprised the Carthaginian general Hanno with his presence there. Hanno sent word to Hasdrubal Barca, who marched north with an army of 8,000 foot soldiers and 1,000 cavalrymen to resist the Romans.[73]

Hanno attacked the Romans near a town called Cissa, though he was outnumbered two to one. Hasdrubal and his relief soldiers were too late to join in and provide support for their fellow Carthaginians, and the battle was, therefore, relatively easy for the Romans. They routed

---

[72] Livius. XXI. 23, 60.

[73] Ibid.

Hanno after killing 6,000 of his soldiers.[74] Gnaeus Scipio captured 2,000 enemy soldiers, the Carthaginian camp, and Hanno.[75]

The Battle of Ticinus

On a flat piece of land on the right bank of the Ticino River in Pavia, Rome and Carthage once more moved into battle positions against one another. This would be the first battle of the Punic Wars that took place on Italian soil, and it was mainly in the hands of the cavalry.

Rome's javelin-throwers had extreme difficulty honing in on their targets once the battle began due to disorganization and the fast pace of the violence. It was the failure of the javelin-throwers to perform that cost Rome the battle, in which consul Scipio was seriously wounded. It was the younger Scipio, merely eighteen years of age, who rescued his father from the battlefield as the Romans retreated. It was a greatly-commended move, since not only was Scipio the Younger looked upon in a much more reverent light afterward, but Rome's army was dependent on the elder Scipio for his leadership and fortitude.

A famous figure in Roman history, Scipio the Elder was included in a historical essay by the 1st-century biographer, Plutarch:

"When somebody inquired in Sicily on what [Scipio] placed his reliance in purposing to take his army across to Carthage, he pointed out to the inquirer three hundred men in armor, who were drilling, and also a lofty tower which overlooked the sea. 'There is not one of these men,' said he, 'who would not go up to the top of that tower and throw himself down head first at my command.'"[76]

---

[74] Ibid.

[75] Lazenby, John Francis. *Hannibal's War*. 1978.

[76] Plutarch. "Apophthegmata Romana."

Scipio took the army to Placentia to rest and regroup while his battle wounds healed. He advised staying away from Hannibal's forces until the winter had passed, but his co-consul, Tiberius Sempronius Longus, was eager to take revenge on the enemy. Hannibal was more than happy to oblige.

The Battle of Trebia River

In fact, Hannibal intended to goad the inexperienced Sempronius into battle while the consuls' armies were camped in different locations. It was the night before the winter solstice when Hannibal marched his army up the Trebia River to Sempronius' camp. There, he told his soldiers to rest and wait for orders in the morning. He also told them that, upon waking, they should cover themselves in fat to help protect themselves from the deep cold.

Mago, the younger brother of Hannibal, was given charge over an ambushing troupe that was intended to attack the Roman lines from behind once the battle began. In the early morning, once the Carthaginian contingents were readied, Hannibal sent members of his Numidian cavalry across the river to taunt and insult Sempronius. Angry and short-sighted, the consul ordered his forces up and to arms without so much as a meal.

Sempronius sent his army across the freezing river in pursuit of the taunting Numidians on foot, and when they reached the far side, they were soaked and shivering. There, they faced off with the Carthaginian army, who was not only well-rested and fed but warm and dry. Even though the Romans outnumbered their enemy, it mattered little as the onslaught of rocks, spears, and javelins bit into their ranks.

Worse, the war elephants under Hannibal's control set to trampling the Romans and slashing them down when they tried to escape back into the river. The final straw was the appearance of Mago's ambush troops, who numbered 2,000 infantry and cavalrymen.[77] Caught up

---

[77] "Battle of the Trebia River." *Encyclopaedia Britannica.* Web.

from the front and rear, an estimated 15,000 Roman soldiers died at the river.[78] As many as that were captured, while a relatively few 5,000 were killed or injured on the Carthaginian side.

Some of the desperate Romans—as many as 10,000—fought all the way through the Carthaginian lines and back to Scipio's encampment at Placentia.[79] They were integrated into Scipio's forces and wintered safely there until the spring.

[78] Ibid.

[79] Ibid.

Chapter Twenty-One – 217 BCE

The Battle of Lake Trasimene

The Romans were defeated soundly once again by the Carthaginians in this second major battle of the Second Punic War, in 217 BCE.[80] Hannibal's Carthaginian army went up against General Gaius Flaminius fighting for the Romans in central Italy at Trasimene, where Hannibal's efforts were strong, and Rome learned the painful lesson of Hannibal's power. At Trasimene, Flaminius' infantry was forced all the way into the lake, where they were either killed as easy targets or drowned, weighed down by their heavy armor.

Flaminius had tried to stop Hannibal by placing his legions at Arretium. He thought this would impede Hannibal's march along the Arno River. Hannibal and his men marched through the wet marshes along the river for four days, and many became sick from it. Hannibal himself got an infection that caused the loss of one eye. Flaminius' failure to attack the Carthaginians when they were most vulnerable and weak ensured his own defeat shortly afterward.

---

[80] Pina Polo, F. *The Consul of Rome.* Cambridge University Press. 2011.

Hannibal placed his men where Flaminius could see their position and then moved them in the night. Flaminius did not send scouts in the morning and relied on his information from the night before. As his forces went forward toward the Carthaginians, Hannibal's forces ambushed them from their new locations.

Flaminius' loss at Trasimene brought him great criticism, and the Romans believed he had rushed into war unprepared.[81]

The Battle of Ager Falernus

Hannibal's army headed south after they'd won the Battle of Lake Trasimene and moved into the river valley of Falernum, which was surrounded by mountains in the region of Campania. Quintus Fabius Maximus Verrucosus was now in command of the Roman field forces. He'd been elected as commander and dictator.

Verrucosus applied a unique strategy to his continued efforts against Hannibal: he only engaged in combat when the conditions were good. He'd been gathering ground and was now in control of all the mountain passes and the river crossings so that the Carthaginians had no way to leave their position at Falernum.

Hannibal's army quickly used up the grains, livestock, and provisions available at Falernum and would need to leave that area to survive. Hannibal managed to employ a clever ploy to remove a Roman guard from their path, and even though they were seen, there was no attack made on them as they escaped.

---

[81] Ibid.

Chapter Twenty-Two – 216 BCE

Rome's armies were not only led by its elected consuls, but by several trusted military generals who had moved up the ranks since their youth as military tribunes. Quintus Fabius Maximus Verrucosus was one of those who served both as a statesman and a military commander during the Second Punic War. Before that, he was a consul in 233 BCE and a censor—a largely administrative office involving finance and running the census.[82] Fabius was one of the few Romans ever to be named dictator; he was appointed this title following Rome's defeat at the hands of Hannibal Barca's army at Lake Trasimene in 217 BCE.[83]

It was as dictator that Fabius earned his most lasting reputation as the great delayer, or in Latin, "Cunctator."[84] Realizing that the Roman Republic needed time to recuperate and regain its strength, Fabius developed the rare wartime strategy of attrition. His plan was

---

[82] "Scipio Africanus." *Encyclopaedia Britannica*. Web.

[83] Ibid.

[84] Ibid.

to wear the enemy down slowly and by secondary means instead of engaging them face to face. Thus, Hannibal's army had nearly free rein throughout Campania, while Fabius directed his own army to stick to the hills, which could not be easily crossed by Hannibal's cavalry and elephants. By maneuvering in this way, the hidden Roman legions cut off the enemy's supply lines and made small-scale attacks to Hannibal's raiding and scouting parties.

Not everyone liked Fabian's tactics, including the commander's own Master of the Horse, Minucius Rufus. With debate ringing through the halls of Rome, the command of the Roman army was eventually split between Fabian and Rufus in 216 BCE.[85] Immediately, Rufus called for direct engagement with Hannibal's army.

The Battle of Cannae

Publius Cornelius Scipio, born in 236 BCE in Campania—now a part of Italy—was born into a wealthy patrician family in Rome as part of a line of men who had all served as consuls and military heroes in their day. Brought up to carry on the family name and reputation, young Scipio began joining his family in military campaigns from the time he was a teenager and young man.

During the conflict between Rome and Numidia in 218 BCE, Scipio's father—of the same name—served as consul and general to the army.[86] At the battle at the Ticinus River, the consul found his army outflanked and in a dangerous position. The younger Scipio acted quickly and boldly, charging forward to engage the enemy so well that his father made a safe retreat with the cavalry. Scipio the younger also escaped unscathed, his actions written down for posterity by the Roman historian, Livy.

---

[85] Mark, Joshua. "Battle of Cannae." *Ancient History Encyclopedia*. Web. 2011.

[86] Ibid.

The next few years were pivotal and turbulent ones for the young man. Serving as a military tribune with the army, Scipio was sent to the Battle of Cannae in 216 BCE, a major engagement of the Second Punic War.[87] It took place in southern Italy, near the town of Cannae, with Rome facing off against Carthage under the leadership of Hannibal. Hannibal came prepared with allies from Africa, the Gallic tribes, and the Celtiberian tribes.

On August 2, 216 BCE, Hannibal Barca and his army arrived at the scene where the battle would take place.[88] Hannibal led an estimated 40,000 infantry soldiers and 10,000 cavalrymen, whose first move was to take control of the Aufidus River. With Carthage in control of the waterway and facing north, Rome's soldiers had significant difficulties restocking their water supplies once they reached the river. Also, since they were forced to face south toward the enemy camp, they dealt constantly with the sun and a gritty, dusty breeze that blew right toward them.

Roman forces, which included the twenty-year-old Scipio, were led by co-consuls Lucius Aemilius Paullus and Gaius Terentius Varro. With no choice but to organize their ranks secondarily to Hannibal's, Paullus and Varro lined up troops in a formation that was deeper than it was wide; this was to deal with the constrictive landscape that Hannibal's own troops did not have to overcome. The consuls were not complicit with Fabian's policy of non-engagement, and they brought as many as 80,000 soldiers with them to Cannae—half of whom were relatively inexperienced in battle.[89]

It was the consuls' plan to meet Hannibal there and take apart his army with a triumphant win, thereby ending the Carthaginian invasion of Italy altogether. It was a bold plan, particularly since the

[87] Ibid.

[88] Ibid.

[89] "Battle of Cannae." *Encyclopaedia Britannica*. Web.

Roman army had arrived last to the site.[90] Nevertheless, the troops—which outnumbered Hannibal's by 10,000 to 40,000—were organized for battle as usual. They faced southwest, the right wing touching the Aufidus River. The 6,000-strong cavalry was placed in the wings, with the infantry making up the mass of the center. Paullus and Varro hoped that the extremely deep and massive infantry would have the raw power necessary to force its way through opposing ranks. It was a classic move for the as-yet underdeveloped Roman military strategy, based almost entirely on overwhelming the enemy with superior numbers. As usual, the consuls hid their heavy infantry behind a line of light infantry, attempting to convince their opponents that they were less of a threat than they were.

Hannibal knew that his own troops, though less in number, had the benefit of more space in which to arrange themselves. Furthermore, he also hid his own heavy infantry behind a line of light infantry. Hannibal put the Gauls and the Spanish tribespeople at the center of his line, as infantry, and two African tribes on their flanks. His cavalry, like that of the Romans, was positioned at both wings. Still more moved further out and reached behind the Roman line.

Rome began the advance, marching forward to engage the Carthaginian lines. When the Romans saw the enemy line retreat, they assumed they were quickly gaining the upper hand. As they continued forward, however, it became clear that Hannibal's light infantry was simply moving back to reveal and flank the heavy infantry hidden behind. Simultaneously, Carthage attacked the Roman cavalry. While Rome relied on its superior numbers, Hannibal had orchestrated a cunning trap. While Rome's back lines could only push the foremost lines ahead, Hannibal's infantry had the space to attack with purpose and dexterity. As the Carthaginian cavalry pushed through Rome's own cavalry, a breach was torn in

---

[90] Ibid. Mark, Joshua. "Battle of Cannae." *Encyclopedia of Ancient History*. Web. 2011.

the line. Hannibal's mounted soldiers poured through, surrounding Rome. The Romans were trapped.

With Hannibal's cavalry at their rear, light infantry at the flanks, and heavy infantry at the front, Paullus and Varro's troops were almost entirely killed. Rome's losses were at least 44,000, with 10,000 soldiers managing to escape to nearby Canusium.[91] Hannibal lost only 6,000 men.[92] The engagement was a complete disaster for the Romans, and for Fabius and his supporters, it seemed like a terrible—and avoidable—waste.

Scipio Regroups

Following the defeat of the Roman army at Cannae, twenty-one-year-old Publius Cornelius Scipio (Scipio the Younger) escaped to Canusium with most of the other survivors.[93] Having seen first-hand the unprecedented military tactics of the enemy, Scipio would remember Hannibal's strategic moves for the rest of his life.

Later, Scipio left the military to pursue a career in government. In 213 BCE, despite being too young to formally take office at the age of twenty-three, Scipio was elected aedile of Rome.[94] As aedile, which translates roughly to "temple edifice" in English, he was responsible for the maintenance and order of the city's public buildings. He was also in charge of maintaining order during public festivals, with the power to enforce public order.

Scipio's father and uncle were both killed at the Battle of the Upper Baetis in 211 BCE.[95] The battle took place in Hispania against

---

[91] Ibid.

[92] Ibid.

[93] "Scipio Africanus." *Encyclopaedia Britannica*. Web.

[94] Ibid.

[95] Mark, Joshua. "Scipio Africanus the Elder." *Ancient History Encyclopedia*. Web. 2011.

Hannibal's brother, Hasdrubal Barca. The two elder Scipios led the Roman army there against Hasdrubal, but despite Rome's established position in Hispania, the victory went to Carthage. With the Roman Republic in need of a new proconsul to lead another army into Hispania, Scipio stepped up, eager to retaliate on the part of his lost family. Again, however, he was underage, only twenty-five years old and therefore too young to take the high office. Despite this, Scipio was unanimously elected by his peers as proconsul of Rome, thereby becoming the primary assistant of the consuls Fulvius Centumalus Maximus and Sulpicius Galba Maximus.

It was a dangerous position that no one else wanted, so with the blessing of the senate, Scipio left Rome with 10,000 infantrymen and 1,000 cavalrymen.[96] In Hispania, Hasdrubal had at least 40,000 troops waiting at Carthago Nova, or New Carthage.[97] Scipio landed at the Ebro River and wasted no time in moving towards the enemy city. Like the original city of Carthage, Carthago Nova was immensely well-defended thanks to a surrounding lagoon and strong fortifications. An entire side of the city's walls were unreachable thanks to the surrounding water.

Thanks to Scipio's intelligence reports, it turned out that this lagoon was probably connected to the sea. Because of this, it was subject to the ebb of the tides and likely to be quite low at certain times of the day. Using this knowledge, Scipio, decided not to rely on the tides of the marsh but instead to drain it altogether. To enact this plan, he sent an attacking force to the front gate of the city to lay siege upon the walls, thereby distracting defenders from the rear. Then, Scipio sent 500 of his soldiers through the drained marsh to climb the walls and gain entry.[98]

---

[96] Ibid.

[97] Ibid.

[98] Ibid.

The plan was a complete success, and Carthago Nova fell to Scipio and the Roman army. The proconsul's troops searched the city for a suitable war prize for their leader and presented Scipio with a woman they said he should take for his bride. Horrified, the girl's family sent ransom money to their conquerors, explaining that she was already engaged to another man and that they were willing to pay for her safe return. Scipio not only sent the girl back to her family, but he returned their ransom money as well. This type of behaviour would come to characterize Scipio's leadership, as he would not condone or participate in any senseless ransacking or violence once battle had come to an end.

Indeed, Scipio the Younger seems to have been a regimented and moral character. A century and a half after the Punic Wars came to an end, the statesman Marcus Tullius Cicero used Scipio as a character in his writings. The following fictional conversation between Scipio and Cato the Wise presents the former as something of a philosopher:

> Scipio: Many a time have I in conversation with my friend Gaius Laelius here expressed my admiration, Marcus Cato, of the eminent, nay perfect, wisdom displayed by you indeed at all points, but above everything because I have noticed that old age never seemed a burden to you, while to most old men it is so hateful that they declare themselves under a weight heavier than Aetna.
>
> Cato: Your admiration is easily excited, it seems, my dear Scipio and Laelius. Men, of course, who have no resources in themselves for securing a good and happy life find every age burdensome. But those who look for all happiness from within can never think anything bad which nature makes inevitable.[99]

---

[99] Marcus Tullius Cicero, Letters of Marcus Tullius Cicero: with his Treatises on Friendship and Old Age, trans. E.S. Shuckburgh. And Letters of Gaius Plinius Caecilius Secundus, trans. William Melmoth, revised by F.C.T. Bosanquet (New York: P.F. Collier, 1909).

Like his father, young Scipio would achieve great things in office and on the battlefield.

The First Battle of Nola

In 216 BCE, after the battle of Cannae, Hannibal attempted to take the town of Nola, near Vesuvius, after marching to Neapolis. Neapolis was allied with Rome, and Hannibal chose not to engage against it. At Nola, he went up against the Romans, who had Marcus Claudius Marcellus at their helm. Marcellus had a larger number of troops than Hannibal did, as he'd gathered up his surviving army from Cannae and added more from Casslinum.

As Marcellus watched Hannibal's moves, he decided to move in toward Nola as well. And, as Hannibal in turn watched Marcellus' moves, he decided to back off from Nola and try to take Neapolis after all. He requested assistance in his battle from Neapolis, but they did not wish to clash with the Romans. The Nolans, however, were uncertain who to support. Nola's senate chose to back Rome, but the people of Nola preferred Hannibal. Marcellus saw Nola as a possible ally for him and put his army there. With no support from Neapolis, Hannibal withdrew to Nuseria. As with Neapolis, he asked Nuseria for their support. They also refused, and in retribution, Hannibal attacked and destroyed their city.

Meanwhile, at Nola, Marcellus had fortified the city and manned the gates of the city with his most adept soldiers. Because Nola did still have some support for Hannibal, Marcellus enacted a law that disallowed civilian people from being near the gates to the city to eliminate any uncontrolled opening and closing of the gates.

When Hannibal and his army reached Nola, they attacked the city walls with rams and ladders to go over the tops of the fortifications. Marcellus surprised Hannibal's men, however, by bursting out of the city gates, breaking through into different parts of the city, and coming back up at them from the flank.

This surprise action accomplished its goal, and the Carthaginians were forced to retreat. The estimates of Hannibal's losses in this first Battle of Nola are anywhere from 5,000 all the way up to 20,000. In any case, it was a devastating loss, and Hannibal retreated from Nola to move his efforts back to the Italian campaign. He went on raiding smaller Roman towns at that point, recruiting more troops and seeking allies in his campaign.

Chapter Twenty-Three – 215 BCE

The Second Battle of Nola

Hannibal returned with his eye on Nola for the second time in 215 BCE. Marcellus was still ensconced at Nola, and his forces were strong there. He and his Roman army had taken to marching out and raiding the surrounding Lucanians, Hirpinians, and Caudine Samnites while occupying Nola. These people were allies of Hannibal, and as they suffered from the Roman raids, they sought his help to bring an end to them.

Hannibal responded to his allies and marched back to Nola not only to avenge his friends but also to launch a new attack that would this time give him the city. Hannibal attempted to take the city using treachery but was unsuccessful. He then assaulted the city. Marcellus and his armies, however, once again provided a strong and quick counterattack on Hannibal there. The battle was strong on both sides, and as a heavy thunderstorm joined in on the action, both sides retreated, with no victors that day.

The next day, the battle would resume. Many of the Carthaginian army who were a part of Hannibal's force had gone off to forage in the area. Marcellus took advantage of Hannibal's minimized ranks and attacked. He'd armed the citizens of Nola and used them as a reserve since he did not have his usual triarii, made of wealthy men with expensive weaponry, on which many Roman battles depended. Marcellus started the battle strongly, but soon the Carthaginians who'd been out foraging heard the assault and quickly returned to take part in the battle against him.

This battle continued for several hours that second day. Both sides were stubbornly engaged, and the fighting held steady with very little maneuvering of either side. Finally, both sides—bloodied and exhausted—retreated from the battlefield, and neither could claim victory or defeat.

Chapter Twenty-Four – 214 BCE

The Third Battle of Nola

In 214 BCE, Hannibal sought to take the city of Nola from the Romans and extend his victories to this place that had been beyond his grasp on two previous occasions.

He'd been expecting Hanno to be successful at Beneventum, which would have given him reinforcements. Hanno was defeated, however, and Hannibal left without a heightened army. He decided to attack Nola for the third time. Nola was still a desirable location, and it would still be a great win for him.

As before, Marcellus and his strong Roman army met Hannibal at Nola. This time, Marcellus had a different strategy than he had the first two battles. He would have Claudius Nero, his legate, march out and come up behind Hannibal while he, Marcellus, would provoke the Carthaginians into battle in the morning.

Morning came, and Marcellus started the battle with Hannibal. The fighting went on for many hours, and Nero never appeared to attack Hannibal from behind. With no sign of Nero, Marcellus withdrew. Nero and his cavalry did return to Nola, having never found their way to the targeted spot behind Hannibal. They'd either gotten lost or, more likely, been unable to make it to their appointed spot within the time allowed for in the planning phase.

Marcellus moved to take up the battle once again the next day, but Hannibal only responded by marching away. This third battle was no more successful than the previous two, and Hannibal finally left Nola to the Romans with no further attempt to make it his own.

The Battle of Beneventum

The Roman legions serving under Tiberius Sempronius Gracchus sought to deal with Hannibal's allies in southern Italy, as they'd put their support with the Carthaginians after the Battle of Cannae.

Gracchus left Lucercia, where he'd spent the winter, and on the order of consul Fabius, set about getting to Beneventum to trap Hannibal in place. He reached his destination about the same time as Hanno did. Hanno had been ordered there by Hannibal for reinforcement. Gracchus took possession of the city easily, mostly because there was already an established Roman garrison there. Camping outside the city, Gracchus was between Hanno's camp about three miles away and the city itself.

Gracchus' troops included two legions of slaves, and, as an incentive to fight hard, the Roman senate now gave the general permission to offer freedom to the slaves if they were successful in this battle against Hanno. Slaves bringing in the head of an enemy would go free.

Both sides, having arrived and camped, readied themselves for battle, which began the next day. Hanno put half his cavalry to his right, at the Calor River, and his infantry in the middle. To his left, he put the other half of his cavalry. Gracchus placed the Roman army with the cavalry on the left and his two legions made up of Romans in the middle between the legions made up of allies.

The promise of freedom for the slaves who were fighting worked somewhat against the Romans as they fought. Rather than slaying the enemy first and then going back later for the heads with which to win their freedom, the slaves were taking the time to decapitate the slain Carthaginians in the middle of the battle. As though that didn't slow them down enough, they then carried the cumbersome heads with them into further battle, slowing them down even more.

Gracchus had to send word to the men engaged in battle that there would be no freedoms won until the enemy was entirely defeated, and they thus found the strength to fight harder.

Meanwhile, Gracchus had his cavalry on the left of Hanno to attack where the Numidian cavalry were.

The Carthaginians were forced back to their camp, and the Roman legions followed and captured the whole camp. They were aided by Roman prisoners there, who'd managed to take up arms and join in the attack. Hanno's army was defeated, and there were fewer than 2,000 men who survived.

While Gracchus was displeased with the performance of many of his soldiers and forced some punishment upon them, the slaves were granted their freedom as promised. Hanno was unable to put together another army for Hannibal, and Gracchus pushed him into Bruttium after the Battle of Beneventum. Hannibal and the Carthaginians were to remain defeated in Campania, and the Romans victorious.

The Siege of Syracuse

In 214 BCE, the Romans turned toward Syracuse once more, having failed time and again in breaching its fortifications. Roman general and proconsul, Marcus Claudius Marcellus, had ordered the siege of Syracuse at the expense of thousands of Roman soldiers and ships. He knew that if this final attempt failed, he would have to retreat. The general also knew the identity of the one man within the city's walls who was making this so difficult on him and his men: the Greek mathematician and engineer, Archimedes.

Archimedes was indeed a formidable man, though not in the normal context of warfare. He approached general philosophy with an assumption that math, physics, engineering, and astronomy were important factors in every subject and event. As the most eminent natural philosopher of his city, Archimedes had a close relationship with the tyrant of Syracuse, Hierro II, and was often called to Hierro's side to help solve complex problems. Thanks to a firm understanding of mathematics and physics, the philosopher invented a ship's pump to remove rainwater, as well as famously contriving a method to calculate the true amount of gold in an oddly-proportioned object.

When Heiro II asked Archimedes to create defensive machines to protect Syracuse, the philosopher complied. Later, when Hierro II died and Syracuse looked to his grandson, Hieronymus, for leadership, Archimedes' defensive devices continued to baffle the Romans. Rome's war with Carthage did nothing to impede its desire to conquer the Sicilian capital.

The Romans had built up their navy in response to continued animosity with Carthage and had become familiar with mechanical tools of seafaring and naval warfare. Still, they were perplexed and frustrated at the barrage of contraptions they faced at Syracuse, including the Claw of Archimedes, impossibly long-range and precise onagers (a type of catapult), and the wall of mirrors.

The Claw of Archimedes was an immense crane with a grappling hook that reached down into the sea. According to the 1st-century Greco-Roman biographer Plutarch, the Claw could lift a ship out of the water and drop it back down, flipping the vessel on its side, capsizing or crushing it. As for the wall of mirrors, this could be arranged and angled to reflect the sunlight and set an enemy ship on fire.

When Roman soldiers finally managed to scale the walls of Syracuse in 212 BCE, it was not due to the failure of these myriads of machines or any particular strategy from Marcellus—it was because the people of Syracuse had become distracted by their Festival of Artemis.[100]

There, they lay siege to the capital city until the tyrant was forced to make peace. Carthage made no move to aid Syracuse, so the results of the Roman siege were that the Sicilian capital became politically allied to its attacker. In the peace treaty, Syracuse pledged to pay a relatively small tax to Rome and also support its army in Sicily. This was the foothold Rome needed to wage war on the remaining Carthaginian holdings within Sicily. Now, the Romans could erect a military base in the interior of the island and overcome their lack of a strong navy. Once Syracuse pledged allegiance to Rome, several small Carthaginian dependencies in Sicily followed suit.

The loss of Syracuse was a huge blow to the Carthaginian efforts, but Hannibal's determination was firm. He would wage war on Rome from within its own territory, stating:

"God has given to man no sharper spur to victory than contempt of death. I will either find a way, or make one. I have come not to make war on the Italians, but to aid the Italians against Rome."[101] "I am not carrying on a war of extermination against the Romans. I am contending for honor and empire. My ancestors yielded to Roman valor. I am endeavoring that others, in their turn, will be obliged to yield to my good fortune, and my valor."[102]

---

[100] Lundquist, Sterling. "How a Mathematician Stopped the Roman Army." *War History Online*. 2019.

[101] Attributed to Hannibal Barca when his generals told him it would be imposible to cross the Alps with an army of elephants.

[102] As quoted in Hannibal: Enemy of Rome (1992) by Leonard Cottrell, p. 150.

Chapter Twenty-Five – 212 BCE

The Night Raid of Tarentum

The Romans were unprepared for Hannibal's arrival at Tarentum in 212 BCE. Marcus Livius was governing the city of Tarentum. Awakened in the night when an alarm was raised, Livius found that Hannibal and his army were already inside the city. There had been drinking and feasting that night, and Hannibal's arrival found many of the Romans drunk and unable to fight.

The Tarentine people themselves were not a Carthaginian target, however. Hannibal allowed his men to loot only from Romans there. He'd had the citizens of Tarentine mark their houses so that they would be spared the pillaging.

The city was no longer under Roman control, but Livius gathered his remaining troops, and they stayed there for the rest of the war. Hannibal moved on to Capua.

The First Battle of Capua

Within days of taking Tarentum, Hannibal faced the Roman consuls Appius Claudius Pulcher and Quintus Fulvius Flaccus at Capua. Hannibal had, in fact, wintered there in 215 BCE. The Capuans had asked Hannibal for his assistance as they found themselves repeatedly being raided by the Romans for supplies since the 214 BCE campaigns.

It was Hanno who came to the aid of the Capuans. He and his army gathered provisions and set up camp close to Beneventum. There was some trouble acquiring the carts needed to take the provisions, however, and the Romans took them while the men were going about the business of foraging for supplies. The Capuans again appealed to Hannibal, and his Numidian cavalry was sent to Capua.

There would be several skirmishes back and forth at Capua, but in the end, the Roman consuls were defeated, and Hannibal was the victor—although life for the Capuans did not benefit greatly from the win.

The Battle of Silarus

In 212 BCE, Marcus Centenius Penula led his Roman army up against Hannibal's Carthaginians in the Battle of Silarus.[103] Hannibal had followed Claudius after the Battle of Capua, but Claudius successfully escaped him. Marcus Centenius Penula had sought the approval of the Roman senate to go after Hannibal independently. He insisted that he was better equipped for the task since he had great knowledge of the area and could defeat the Carthaginians in a way no one else could.

Centenius was granted his request and was given an army of 8,000 for his effort. Half of the troops were citizen soldiers, and the other half were allies. His numbers swelled with volunteers, and in total he commanded 16,000 men.

When Hannibal discovered the Romans were approaching, though, he abandoned his pursuit of Claudius. He used his cavalry to secure the roads as a means of stopping the retreat of the Romans. The two sides engaged in battle as soon as they saw each other, and while the

---

[103] Yardley, J.C. *Hannibal's War – Livius*. Oxford University Press. 2006.

Romans held for two hours, once Centenius was killed, they fell. Nearly 15,000 Romans and their allies died in the Battle of Silarus. Only 1,000 of those who survived made it past the blockades Hannibal's cavalry had set up.

Victorious, Hannibal headed east into Apulia rather than continue the pursuit of Claudius.

Chapter Twenty-Six – 211 BCE

The Battle of Upper Baetus

During the Second Punic War, in 211 BCE, the Battle of Upper Baetis in Spain was fought. This was actually a double-faceted battle, with the Carthaginian armies up against the Scipio brothers in a battle at Castulo and at Ilorca.

Gnaeus Cornelius Scipio Calvus and Publius Cornelius Scipio had taken the city of Castulo, a successful mining town that was important to their cause. They once again needed to replenish their troops after losses to the Carthaginians and the Iberian tribes had reduced their number to only 20,000. So, they began hiring mercenaries to strengthen their Roman army. Most of these new troops were Celtiberians.

The Scipio brothers decided to divide and conquer in this case, and Gnaeus took a third of their army and the mercenaries off to deal with Hasdrubal Barca near Ilorca. Publius took the remainder of the Roman army and their allies off to Castulo to engage with Mago Barca. The resulting Battle of Castulo and the Battle of Ilorca took place within days of each other.

Gnaeus and his forces reached their destination first. Iberian chieftains who were allied with the Carthaginians had already been ordered in by Hasdrubal Barca. The Romans were thwarting any of their efforts to gain ground, however, and Hasdrubal's forces remained inside their fortified encampment. However, the tides soon turned for Gnaeus once the Celtiberian mercenaries were bribed to desert their allegiance to the Scipios. Once the mercenaries abandoned the Roman army, Hasdrubal and his army outnumbered their opponents.

Once Hasdrubal Gisco and Mago Barca arrived, Gnaeus decided that with his greatly reduced numbers, withdrawing to the north of Iberia would be the best option. They left their camp in the night with their campfires still alight and headed to the Ebro River. They were found the next day by the Numidians and were attacked, forcing them to settle for the night on a hill near Ilorca. During that night, the Carthaginian forces of Hasdrubal Barca, Hasdrubal Gisco, and Mago Barco all showed up to face the Romans. The Romans erected a wall with what they had to try to protect themselves, but their saddles and baggage wall was of little use. As they were also greatly outnumbered, the battle was easily won by the Carthaginians. Gnaeus Scipio was killed in battle, and there was little left of his army afterward.

Publius and his men, who had set off to Castulo, found themselves being harassed by Masinissa's Numidian cavalry during their journey. Publius also learned that there were some 7,500 Iberians moving across his path. He feared the Carthaginians and their allies would surround him, so he decided to attack the Iberian chieftain in a move calculated to give himself some working room. He left 2,000 of his soldiers at camp with his legate Tiberius Fonteus and, in the night, marched out with hopes of evading Masinissa. He caught Indibilis the chieftain by surprise early the next morning. Scipio's Roman forces outnumbered the Iberians and, at first, took control. Unfortunately for Scipio, the Iberians managed to hold up long enough for Masinissa to arrive and join them.

Once Masinissa's Numidian cavalry was attacking the Romans from their flank, the Iberians found some relief. Mago and Hasdrubal

Gisco also arrived from their victory over the other Scipio brother, and soon the Romans were defeated. Publius Scipio was also killed at the hands of the Carthaginians, along with most of his men.

Mago allowed the Numidians some time to loot the dead Romans and then marched them off toward Hasdrubal Barca. There were very few Romans who survived this battle, and the double-ended Battle of Baetus was the only time the Carthaginians won against the Romans in the Second Punic War without Hannibal at their helm. The Scipio brothers had fought for seven years, campaigning for Rome.

The Second Battle of Capua

There would be a second siege at Capua only a year after the first when the Romans again tried to take the city before Hannibal could return.[104] Hannibal was in the southern part of Italy at the time, and the Romans figured he would be too far away to respond to their attack.

Hannibal responded by instead attacking Rome directly. He assumed the Romans would simply flee Capua again once he got close and take up their siege when he left again. Attacking Rome would cause the army to leave Capua to get back to Rome, where he would engage them in battle.

The Roman forces at Capua did not respond as Hannibal expected, however. They did not march back to Rome to fight him. Also, Rome's defenses were far stronger than Hannibal could break. He had fewer men and supplies than would have been necessary to make any significant assault on Rome. Meanwhile, Capua fell to the Romans.

---

[104] Brice, L. Warfare in the Roman Republic. ABC-CLIO. 2014

The loss was the end of Capua. Rome was not kind to those who survived there; it became a Roman territory that later was divided, and parts were sold.

Chapter Twenty-Seven – 210 BCE

The Battle of Numistro

Hannibal and his Carthaginian army met the Roman army under Marcus Claudius Marcellus in 210 BCE at the Battle of Numistro.[105] These two had clashed in battle previously near Nola in 216, 215, and 214 BCE. Marcellus had generally been more successful than Hannibal.

The Battle of Numistro only lasted for one day. It was a hard battle, and by nightfall, it was over, but its outcome was a draw. Hannibal retreated to Apulia the day after, and Marcellus went after him. In the meantime, the Roman soldiers were left behind to recover from their injuries.

Hannibal and Marcellus would clash again within months at Canusium.

---

[105]

Livius "Ab Urbe Condita" XXVII,2

The Battle of Canusium

The Romans were still trying to restrict Hannibal's grasp in the south of Italy. In the summertime of 209 BCE, the Carthaginian army under Hannibal once again faced the Romans under Marcus Claudius Marcellus. This time it was at Apulia.

At the time, the Romans were vengefully punishing the tribes that had opposed them or had broken alliances with them. They also targeted cities that had stood against their forces throughout their drive to expand.

During the three days that the Battle of Canusium covered, Hannibal hoped to regain his hold on the area, and Marcellus hoped to stop it completely. Hannibal's Carthaginian army took up camp near Canusium. They endeavored to gain the support of the Canusium people, who were currently allied with the Romans. Hannibal was well aware that the Numidians in a nearby location had been betrayed by their Roman allies, and Marcellus had ordered their deaths only a year previous.

The Carthaginians were not able to hold Canusium, however, and Hannibal moved his army back, hoping to ambush Marcellus. There were battles throughout the day, but by that night, both sides had fallen back to their camps.

The following day, Hannibal's army defeated Marcellus' Roman army by continuing forward once one of the Roman wings had lost its ground. Marcellus moved his legion around to cover for his allies who were in retreat, but the Carthaginians pressed forward.

On the last day of the three-day battle, the Romans fought back hard despite their losses the previous day. That is until Hannibal brought his war elephants, which sent the Romans scurrying off in all directions as they tried not to get trampled. Unfortunately for Hannibal, however, there was a move that sent the animals back onto the Carthaginians. Marcellus then sent his cavalry out along with the infantry, and Hannibal and his men were forced back to their camp after losing 8,000 men. The Romans had suffered tremendous losses, as well, over the three days, and Marcellus chose not to go after Hannibal any longer.

Hannibal continued through that summer with no more trouble from the Romans, and Marcellus headed back to Campania. He faced criticism from Rome after this battle but was elected again and tasked with the continued battle against Hannibal.

Chapter Twenty-Eight – 209 BCE

The Assault on New Carthage

New Carthage was the Carthaginian stronghold in Hispania, founded in 227 BCE by Hasdrubal the Fair.[106] Mostly hidden in a bay and surrounding on three sides by water, the location was ideal in terms of defense. In the winter of 210 BCE, the Roman commander Publius Cornelius Scipio sailed to Hispania and spent the season organizing his army for a surprise attack on New Carthage.[107] Since warfare was almost always staged in the warm months, the Carthaginians would have expected the Romans to be away at their winter camps. Instead, Scipio amassed 30,000 troops and readied them for a fight.[108]

It was a bold move, considering that three Carthaginian generals were also in Hispania at the time: Hasdrubal Barca, Mago Barca, and Hasdrubal Gisco. These were quite far apart, however, with Barca at the center of the country, Mago near Gibraltar, and Hasdrubal at the

---

106 Livius. *Hasdrubal the Fair.*

107 Livius. 26, 44.

108 Ibid.

Tagus River. Furthermore, the generals were on poor terms with one another and were struggling to create a concise battle plan.

Though New Carthage was in wintering mode, there were 1,000 soldiers stationed there, and 2,000 civilians prepared to defend the gates of the city.[109] Coordinating with the Roman fleet, which was commanded by Gaius Laelius, Scipio cut off the city via the small strip of land on its eastern edge, while Laelius moved in the navy to block supplies and aid via the sea. Between the two Roman sides, New Carthage was completely trapped. Working quickly, Scipio besieged the city without bothering to set up a defensive line against any Carthaginian allies that might creep up from the east to help the city. Carthage's allies were only about ten days away, which meant that Scipio and Laelius had to make very short work of the city's defenses.

On land, Scipio attacked across the isthmus, while the navy attacked from the southern side. The Carthaginians fought fiercely, civilians included, to break the siege engines of their Roman enemies. About 2,000 armed citizens flooded out of the city's eastern gate to wreak havoc on the machines before moving on toward the Roman camp.[110] The counter-attack was so fearsome that Scipio was forced to call in his reserve troops to beat them back into a retreat. Even then, spears continued to fly at the Romans, who took heavy casualties and retreated temporarily to regroup.

Later in the day, the siege continued alongside a stealthy assault from the lagoon on the north side of the city. Fortuitously for the Romans, a wind storm moved some of the lagoon's waters into the sea, making it easier for the northern raiding group to press through. Once across the lagoon, soldiers crested the northern wall of New Carthage and attacked the defenders from the rear. From the sea,

---

[109] Ibid.

[110] Goldsworthy, Adrian. *The Punic Wars*. 2000.

Roman ships pressed into the south edge of the city and lay siege there, as well.

The historian Polybius described the brutal way in which Scipio stormed New Carthage:

"Directed according to the Roman custom, against the people in the city, [Scipio told] them to kill everyone they met and to spare no one, and not to start looting until they received the order. The purpose of this custom is to strike terror. Accordingly, one can see in cities captured by the Romans not only humans who have been slaughtered, but even dogs sliced in two and the limbs of other animals cut off. On this occasion the amount of such slaughter was very great."

Chapter Twenty-Nine– 208 BCE

The Battle of Baecula

At the Battle of Baecula in 208 BCE, Publius Cornelius Scipio (the Younger) used the very same military tactics on Hannibal's army that he had learned from the enemy at the Battle of Cannae.[111]

It was important that Scipio pre-empted the armies of his enemies coming together to form one large, strong force against him. Since the armies of the Carthaginians were spread some distance apart, he strategized to attack each of them individually rather than wait for them to assemble en masse against his efforts.

He brought with him 30,000 Roman and Italian soldiers, as well as some 10,000 auxiliary troops from Spain. With what had been taken in New Carthage, Scipio bolstered his army with more heavy weapons. He increased his manpower with the men from the ships that had been used to take the Spanish coast into Roman command. With that completed, these men were now available for the next battle.

---

[111] Ibid.

His army now replenished with weaponry and men, Scipio went in search of Hasdrubal and his army in 208 BC.[112] Hasdrubal was found near Baecula, where he and his 30,000 men had spent the winter near the Baetis River.[113] The Carthaginian camp was set up with cavalry sentinels. However, when Scipio's army attacked, they took these sentinels quickly, leaving the Carthaginians unprepared for battle. The Carthaginians were driven back as the Romans kept up the onslaught until they were within the enemy's camp, where Scipio set up for the night.

Hasdrubal retreated to a flat-topped hill near the Baecula River, where the terrain provided some security, and set up camp there. The plateau south of Baecula was high with steep sides, and the river and ravines provided security. Hasdrubal used the stepped plateaus by stationing his light troops on the lower ground and putting his main camp behind it.

As Scipio rallied his men for the next battle, he reminded them that the walls of New Carthage had been higher than the hill they now faced. It was a hard fight up the hill as the Carthaginians assailed them with missiles. Scipio's army made it up that hill, and once they had, the flat plateau provided them a strong win with hand-to-hand combat. The upper plateau of the hill was where Scipio was aiming, however. He sent Gaius Laelius and half his men off to make their way to the right side of the hill while he and the rest of his men went around to the left. From there, the Romans surprised the Carthaginians from the side, and Laelius and his men arrived on the plateau, as well.

The details of this battle were related by Polybius in his writings: "On this occasion Scipio appears to have employed a two-fold

---

[112] Hoyos, Dexter (2015). Mastering the West: Rome and Carthage at War. Oxford: Oxford University Press.

[113] Strauss, Barry. "Masters of Command: Alexander, Hannibal, Caesar, and the Genius of Leadership". Simon and Schuster. 2012

strategem. Hasdrubal had been accustomed to make his demonstrations in force somewhat late in the day, with the Libyans in his centre, and the elephants on either wing; while his own practice had been to make his counter movements somewhat later still, with the Roman soldiers on his centre opposite the Libyans, and the Iberians on his two wings; but the day on which he resolved upon a general engagement by reversing this arrangement, he greatly contributed to secure the victory for his own men, and succeeded in putting the enemy at a considerable disadvantage. For directly it was light he sent his aides with orders to the tribunes and men to arm, as soon as they had got their breakfasts, and parade outside the camp. The order was obeyed with alacrity because the men suspected what was going to take place. He then sent the cavalry and light-armed forward, with orders to advance close to the enemy's camp, and skirmish boldly up to it; while he himself marched out with the infantry, just as the sun was appearing above the horizon; and on reaching the middle of the plain, made his dispositions in the reverse order to his usual arrangement, placing the Iberians in the centre and the Roman legionaries on the two wings."[114]

The battleground on the plateau was a chaotic mass of men, horses, and elephants. Polybius' account said, "When these troops were at close quarters the elephants were severely handled, being wounded and harassed on every side by the velites and cavalry, and did as much harm to their friends as to their foes; for they rushed about promiscuously and killed every one that fell in their way on either side alike."[115]

As the Romans put their efforts into plundering the Carthaginian camp rather than locating Hasdrubal, he managed to escape. As

---

[114] Shuckburgh, Evelyn S., Histories of Polybius – Translated from the Text of F. Hultsch. Macmillan and Company, 1889.

[115] Ibid

many as 12,000 Carthaginians were taken prisoner by the Romans, and 8,000 men lost their lives. Most of the losses were Hasdrubal's Iberian allies and the light troops who had been positioned on the lower plateau. Hasdrubal retreated toward the Pyrenees to regroup and rebuild. He managed to keep his elephants, a few men, and much of his baggage as he left Baecula.

After the Battle of Baecula, Scipio endeavored to reward Indibilis for his defection to the Roman side with 300 horses that had been captured in the battle. In a gesture of clemency, he also returned to Prince Masinissa a captive prisoner who was a relative. Scipio, while a fearsome strategist and warrior, was at the same time noted for his humanity. Scipio, who was eminently endowed by nature in this respect conducted himself with so much kindness and tact that Hasdrubal afterward remarked to Syphas that "Scipio appeared more formidable to him in such an interview than in the field."[116] In Scipio's own words, "I am mindful of human weakness, and I reflect upon the might of Fortune and know that everything that we do is exposed to a thousand chances."[117]

---

[116] Ibid

[117] Livius, Titus. The History of Rome Book 30. James Brodie. 1968.

Chapter Thirty – 207 BCE

The Battle of Metaurus

The next engagement was near the Metauro River in Italy. Hasdrubal Barca led the Carthaginians, while the Roman legions were led by consuls Marcus Livius and Gaius Claudius Nero. Nero was already leading an army several hundred kilometers south of the Metaurus, having faced off victoriously against Hannibal in Grumentum. Intent on joining the battle in the north, Nero marched the weary army northward and was completely undetected by either Hannibal or Hasdrubal.

Upon meeting up with consul Livius' army, the combined Roman legions outnumbered the Carthaginians and succeeded in routing the opposing forces. The Carthaginians' elephants and Hispanic allies were also forced to flee. Among the more than 14,000 soldiers killed or captured on the Carthaginian side, Hasdrubal lost his life.[118]

Hamilcar refused to admit defeat in Italy despite the death of Hasdrubal and the fact that the Carthaginian survivors had mostly fled or been captured. He persisted, gathering an army of 40,000 to

---

[118] Hoyos, Dexter. *Hannibal's Dynasty: Power and politics in the western Mediterranean, 247–183 BC*. 2003.

mount an attack on the Roman territory of Cisalpine Gaul, to the north of mainland Italy.[119] This, too, was unsuccessful, though a small contingent of Carthaginian soldiers remained in Cisalpine Gaul for several years afterward, sporadically harassing the Romans there.

---

[119] Griffith, Guy Thompson. *The Mercenaries of the Hellenistic World.* 1933.

Chapter Thirty-One – 206 BCE

The Battle of Ilipa

The Carthaginians were camped near Esquivel in Spain, and Scipio plotted to engage them in battle in hopes of breaking their hold in Iberia. Cutting the Carthaginians off from Italy at Esquivel was thought to be the best way to make them leave. Without the silver, the land, and the men they took from Italy, they would find it difficult to stay.

Hanno and Mago Barca combined forces in Iberia and put together a large army, which again included Celtiberian mercenaries. Hasdrubal Gisco had also brought his army up, so the Romans faced two forces. Scipio was loath to let one of them get behind him, which is what would happen if he attacked the other.

Scipio decided to send Marcus Silanus and a detachment of men to make a strike on Mago. They took great haste in getting to Mago and surprising him. They were successful and, in fact, captured Hanno himself, causing the allied mercenaries to flee.

This meant the Romans could now deal with Hasdrubal's forces without facing Hanno's at the same time, but as it turned out, they didn't need to. Hasdrubal managed to divide his men up between two fortified cities and thus did not have to go into further battle at the time.

In the spring, though, the Carthaginians made another attempt to regain what they'd held in Iberia. Hasdrubal Gisco and Mago came together at Ilipa and, with their combined forces of somewhere between 50,000 and 70,000 men, were now large enough to face Scipio again.

Mago began by sending Masinissa, his Numidian friend with cavalry, in to attack the camp of the Romans. Scipio was not surprised and, with his Roman cavalry hidden until the flank of the Carthaginians was clear, his attack was effective. For the next few days, both sides spent most of their time watching each other. The Romans consistently remained unmoved until the Carthaginians left their camp and always presented themselves in the same formation, with the Iberians on either side and the legions in the middle.

Mago and Hasdrubal now mistakenly expected this same formation from the Romans. Once he'd successfully convinced his foes of this habit, however, Scipio changed it up. He had his men fed before daybreak, sent the cavalry to the outer Carthaginian posts, and took his men forward. This time, the Iberians took up the center, and the legions were at the wings. They pressed forward straight toward the enemy camp.

The Carthaginians were taken by surprise and had to ready themselves for battle without breakfast, still basing their formation on Scipio's previous actions, which were a ruse. Hasdrubal was unable to change his formation once he realized the Romans had changed their position this time. It was too late, and the battle began near his camp. Scipio held his infantry back until the Carthaginians had fought for several hours and would now be feeling the full effect of having missed breakfast.

The wings of the Carthaginian formation could not hold up, and with their demise, the center soon had their own elephants driven towards them by the Romans, who were closing in on the sides. Scipio's forces were surrounding the Carthaginians while they became exhausted and hungry. The Carthaginians began to withdraw from battle. Luckily for them, the skies opened into a downpour, which allowed them to seek cover in their camp as the fighting suddenly ended. They were not safe there for long, however, as they would face another attack in the morning. The Spanish mercenaries were not motivated to stay and began to desert as night fell, and Hasdrubal realized he should move his men out in the darkness, as well.

Scipio's Roman army went after them and brutally slew most of the Carthaginian force that was left. However, Hasdrubal and Mago managed to flee with their remaining men and took up camp on a mountain. From there, Hasdrubal and Mago fled completely and left their men with no water. The soldiers didn't last long before surrendering to the Romans.

Before he left Iberia, Scipio saw to it that the chieftains of Iberia received punishment for their betrayal, which had previously caused the deaths of his father and uncle. The Carthaginians had no further hold in Iberia, and Scipio could finally return to Rome, where he would now be elected consul and given control of Sicily.

Chapter Thirty-Two – 205-204 BCE

The Battle of Crotan

With Hannibal in Bruttium, Rome's goal was to keep him blockaded from the Ionian Sea and subsequent passage back to Carthage. To facilitate this extended blockade, Rome sought to capture the city of Croton in southern Italy. Hannibal had been using the city as winter quarters for his army for three years, and Rome was not only eager to capture their enemy but to take back their city. It would be a very difficult campaign, however, since Bruttium was a mountain region surrounded by the sea and made for an excellent natural fortress.

The Roman Senate elected Scipio as consul for 205 BCE, along with Publius Licinius Crassus. The Senate accepted Scipio's word that major warfare was necessary in Africa to lure Hannibal out of Italy. Not only was Hannibal established in Bruttium, but the Carthaginians had a second foothold in Italy by way of Liguria. Though the senate agreed with Scipio's plan, they did not give him all the resources he asked for, which delayed the battle significantly.

Unable to set out for Bruttium directly, Scipio spent about a year gathering more numbers for his army and putting together an arsenal of weapons and supplies. Meanwhile, the existing army made multiple unsuccessful attempts to break into the Carthaginian camps there.

The historian Livius had this to say of the situation:

"The struggle in Bruttium had assumed the character of brigandage much more than that of regular warfare. The Numidians had commenced the practice, and the Bruttians followed their example, not so much because of their alliance with the Carthaginians as because it was their traditional and natural method of carrying on war. At last, even the Romans were infected by the passion for plunder and, as far as their generals allowed them, used to make predatory incursions on the enemy's fields."[120]

Hannibal was awaiting help from Carthage, but the 100-ship fleet full of soldiers and supplies never arrived, having been driven off course by high winds and then intercepted by Roman vessels at Sardinia.[121] Desperate, Hannibal resorted to confiscating what he needed from the surrounding communities, as well as raising taxes within Bruttium. With these actions, the general's popularity plummeted, and many of his people in Italy defected.

During the late part of 205 BCE, an infectious disease swept through Italy, weakening and killing many Carthaginians, as well as Romans.[122] It was worse for Hannibal and his allies in Bruttium, however, since they were already dealing with a food shortage. The disease was so rampant and debilitating that consul Crassus could not go back to Rome for the next year's consular elections and instead asked the Senate to call one of the armies home to preserve

---

[120] Livius. XXIX, 6.

[121] Appian, Hannibalic War, VIII, 54.

[122] Livius. XXVIII, 46.

the soldiers' lives. The Senate gave Crassus its permission to recall an army, so the next year's consul, Publius Sempronius Tuditanus, had to bring fresh troops when he visited Bruttium to lead the charge.

The Romans and Carthaginians began to clash once more in 204 BCE, though after one skirmish, Sempronius was convinced that his legions were no match for the enemy lines. The next night, he snuck out of camp under cover of darkness to meet with Crassus and summon his aide. Crassus agreed, and the two returned to Croton with Crassus' troops in tow, intent on finally routing Hannibal and the Carthaginians from the tip of Italy.

The combined forces of both Roman consuls outnumbered those of Hannibal, with Sempronius' legions arranged in formation and those of Crassus lined up as reserves in the rear. The Romans forced the Carthaginians troops to retreat from the hinterlands into the city of Croton, where they sheltered. Though they did not take Croton itself, the Romans did conquer the surrounding communities, which were allied with Hannibal. Some of these cities and towns surrendered willingly to the consuls without any need for a fight.

Ultimately, however, Hannibal could not be ousted from Croton. The Carthaginian fleet eventually met him there, and he constructed more ships to join their ranks.

The Siege of Utica

In 204 BCE, Scipio set his sights on Utica. He saw it as a good resource from which to obtain necessary supplies as he continued his campaigns against the Carthaginians. When he and his forces arrived near Utica, the Carthaginians in the countryside were afraid and moved into the nearby towns for protection. Hasdrubal Gisco was sent into action, and there was a request for assistance from Syphax.

While Scipio attempted several times to assault the city of Utica to gain supplies, he remained unsuccessful, and the city held strong. After forty days of this, Hasdrubal Gisco and his Carthaginian army, as well as the Numidian King Syphax (who was Hasdrubal's son-in-law) and his army, arrived. Scipio abandoned his goal there and retreated.

Scipio moved inland and carried on a campaign to pillage the farms of everything useful and then burn them. He captured a ridgeline of hills and set up outposts, where he fortified his position and settled in for the winter.

Hanno was sent to take stock of the situation and to harass Scipio's forces. The Roman cavalry defeated Hanno's men, and Hanno himself was killed. The Romans continued to take nearby towns and raid the farms for supplies and valuables they could send back to Sicily. They took as many as 8,000 Carthaginians and moved them to Sicily as hostages.

Chapter Thirty-Three – 203-202 BCE

The Battle of Bagbradas

Also known as the Battle of the Great Plains, this encounter took place near the upper Bagradas River on the plains of North Africa. The belligerents were a combined Carthaginian and Numidian army under the leadership of Hasdrubal Gisco and Syphax against the Roman army under Scipio. This battle was designed by Rome as a diversionary tactic, which would hopefully—this time—alarm the Carthaginians enough to withdraw Hannibal from Italy.

Hasdrubal Gisco and Syphax were joined by a faction of Hispanic mercenaries, mainly Celts, who were placed at the center of the formation. These were flanked by Carthage's own infantry and cavalry. The Roman formation consisted of a triple line, in which the hastati were in front, principes in the center, and triarii at the rear. Triarii were made up of wealthy men who could afford heavy armor and shields, and these were armed with spears. The hastate were poorer, outfitted in light chain mail with short swords or spears. Principes were generally spearmen or swordsmen in heavier armor.

Rome made the charge starting with their cavalry, which routed most of the Carthaginian infantry and cavalry. The Spanish mercenaries held their ground better, fighting fiercely against an equal number of first-line Romans. Scipio ordered his second and third line to flank the mercenaries, overwhelming them and sending them fleeing. Only a small number of the Hispanics managed to escape. That left Syphax and the Numidians in the fight, but without their allies, it was a lost cause and a wasted effort. They, too, fled.

Syphax made a retreat with his army all the way back to Numidia, but Masinissa and Laelius followed him, unwilling to let him escape. At the subsequent Battle of Cirta, Rome and Numidia were victorious in capturing Syphax and shipping him to Rome as a prisoner of war. Masinissa was given command of Numidia in Syphax's place, a fitting tribute as he was an exile of that land.

The Battle of Zama

In 203 BCE, Carthage found itself in great danger. Roman general Publius Cornelius Scipio had crossed the Mediterranean into North Africa the year before, adding to his army. Scipio had already engaged with the Carthaginians at Utica, winning an important battle that placed him nearer than ever to Carthage itself. There, Scipio allied with the Numidian king, Masinissa. Hannibal and his brother Mago were, at long last, recalled from their missions in Italy to return home and protect Carthage. Hannibal came home with 12,000 veteran soldiers and had soon grown the army to an estimated 37,000.[123] Mago died at sea en route to Carthage, having been fatally wounded in battle before embarking on the voyage.[124]

In pressing towards Carthage and causing Hannibal to be recalled from Italy, Scipio achieved exactly what he wanted. Hannibal had been campaigning in Italy for twelve years by then, devastating much of what belonged to Rome and its allies there.[125] With

---

[123] Hunt, Patrick. "Battle of Zama." *Encyclopaedia Britannica*. Web.

[124] Hunt, Patrick. "Battle of Zama." *Encyclopaedia Britannica*. Web.

[125] Mark, Joshua. "The Battle of Zama." *Encyclopedia of Ancient History*. Web. 2011.

Hannibal back in Africa, Scipio wanted to engage him at Carthage, knowing that Italy was enjoying a much-needed reprieve.

For his part, Scipio marched determinedly towards Carthage along the Bagradas River with several thousand survivors of the Battle of Cannae behind him. Once allies and reinforcements joined the ranks, Scipio had an estimated 40,000 soldiers on his side.[126] Of these, 6,100 were cavalrymen led by the Numidian ruler Masinissa and the Roman general Gaius Laelius. These were highly-trained cavalry, and they were expected to make a significant difference in the coming battle.

As for Hannibal, he had been unable to transport most of his horses to Carthage from Italy, which meant that his own cavalry numbered only 4,000.[127] Not wishing to leave the horses in Italy where the Romans could easily add them to their own cavalry, Hannibal had all un-transportable horses slaughtered. His were mostly from his own Numidian ally, whose name was Tychaeus. At Zama, the two generals met once more.

As always, Hannibal had a regiment of war elephants with him, numbering about 80.[128] These were not, however, fully trained. Furthermore, of his 40,000 troops, only about 12,000-15,000 of them had real battle experience against the Romans. The rest were recruited from Carthage to support the experienced veterans and bulk up the numbers. As the two sides faced off, Hannibal put his veterans near the rear of his formation. Before the first strike was made, the two generals met face to face to discuss terms. Hannibal apparently proposed a settlement, but it did not satisfy Scipio, who replied that Carthage had broken the terms of their earlier truce and, therefore, must be forced to pay the consequences.

---

[126] Ibid.

[127] Ibid.

[128] Ibid.

Roman historian Livius documented the discourse that took place between the leaders of the two great armies. Scipio, he wrote, gave his enemy the following advice:

"Prepare to fight because evidently you have found peace intolerable."[129]

Negotiations having failed, each general stalked away to his own camp, vowing to fight the next day. It was October 19 when they threw themselves into battle.[130] Hannibal's first order was to set the war elephants loose upon the Roman infantry. Though this made for chaos and fear in the short-term, the elephants' lack of training meant that the Romans were soon able to force them out of the fray altogether. The trumpet communications of war, coupled with the screams and shouts of both armies, frightened many of the elephants away, in some cases causing them to attack their own ranks.

Furthermore, anticipating the use of elephants, Scipio had trained his soldiers for just such an attack. When an elephant stampeded toward the line, the Romans quickly pivoted, forming alleys of shield walls through which the animals could run. When the elephants had moved on and exited the formation, the troops pivoted back to face the enemy lines once more. When Scipio's forces had dealt properly with the elephants, the cavalry charged.

Indeed, the superior training of Masinissa's cavalry had exactly the right effect on Hannibal's hastily organized riders. The latter quickly fled, leaving the field open for Rome's infantry to move in on that of the Carthaginians. Rome's offensive lines moved through the first and second defensive lines, finally revealing the third, veteran infantry line under Hannibal's command. The veterans proved the toughest of all Hannibal's army that day, and with Rome's

---

[129] Hunt, Patrick. "Battle of Zama." *Encyclopaedia Britannica*. Web.

[130] "19th October 202 BC." *HistoryPod*. Web. 2019.

infantrymen heartily exhausted already, this part of the battle marked a crucial point.

Having routed the enemy cavalry, Masinissa and his riders returned in time to attack Hannibal's remaining infantry from the rear. With the combined efforts of the cavalry and the Roman infantry, Hannibal's third line was caught between the two. With nowhere to go, it crumbled, giving victory to Rome. The death toll for Carthage was 20,000; for Rome, 1,500.[131] Another 20,000 Carthaginian hostages were captured by Scipio.[132]

Roman historian Cornelius Nepos gave the battle its name 150 years after the fact, but the exact site has never been identified.[133] Rome's victory at the Battle of Zama left Carthage utterly without defense, and thus it made immediate efforts to solidify a peace agreement with Scipio. Rome demanded the return of Hispania to its own authority, and Carthage had no choice but to hand it over. Further terms of surrender called for Carthage to surrender the bulk of its warships, some of which were publicly burned. As to indemnity payments, Carthage was required to pay an annual sum of 10,000 silver talents for fifty years.[134] That was three times as much as had been demanded at the end of the First Punic War.

When he finally returned to Carthage, Scipio did not punish Hannibal but allowed him to be elected as a civil magistrate. It was a tactic that Rome would learn to use again and again as its empire expanded. Using defeated leaders to help administrate new Roman cities and provinces proved one of the best ways to rule over a conquered people.

---

[131] Hunt, Patrick. "Battle of Zama." *Encyclopaedia Britannica*. Web.

[132] Ibid.

[133] Hunt, Patrick. "Battle of Zama." *Encyclopaedia Britannica*. Web.

[134] Ibid.

Chapter Thirty-Four – 183-180 BCE

Hannibal's Death

Though the Romans had given Hannibal an important role in the administration of Carthage following the Second Punic War, his allegiance to Rome was born of necessity. Whether he conspired with enemies of Rome is not known for certain; however, clearly the Romans accused him of such conspiracy in 195 BCE. Aware of the danger he was in, Hannibal fled Carthage and put himself into self-exile in Ephesus, where he was warmly welcomed by the Macedonian King Antiochus. Ironically, Antiochus wished to discuss the best way to wage war on Rome—and Hannibal was happy to take up the subject.

Eventually, Hannibal found himself in the service of Prusias I of Bithynia, who was at war with King Eumenes II of Pergamon, one of Rome's allies. In time, he became paranoid that Prusias was planning to turn him over to the Romans, so he fled once more. Despite several histories on the subject, the year and exact cause of Hannibal's death are disputed. The following was written by the 2nd-century Roman historian, Pausanias:

Hannibal received an oracle from Ammon that when he died he would be buried in Libyan earth. So, he hoped to destroy the Roman empire, to return to his home in Libya, and there to die of old age. But when Flamininus the Roman was anxious to take him alive, Hannibal came to Prusias as a suppliant. Repulsed by Prusias he jumped upon his horse, but was wounded in the finger by his drawn sword. [The] wound caused a fever, and he died on the third day. The place where he died is called Libyssa by the Nicomedians.[135]

---

[135] Pausanias. *Pausanias Description of Greece*, with an English Translation by W.H.S. Jones, Litt.D., and H.A. Ormerod, M.A., in 4 Volumes. Cambridge, MA, Harvard University Press; London, William Heinemann Ltd. 1918.

Chapter Thirty-Five – 150 BCE

Carthage Breaks the Peace Treaty with Rome

An important feature of the peace treaty between Carthage and Rome was the fact that the former was not allowed to use force and arms against the latter. When the Roman ally, Masinissa, tried to gain control over the booming Carthaginian trade industry, however, Carthage reacted with weapons. It was technically an act of war against Rome itself, so once more, the legions moved into North Africa and made ready to lay siege to Carthage.

Hastily, Carthage moved to make things right with the Roman Republic. They sent 300 hostages into Roman hands and gave up their weapons, which worked for a short time. Soon, however, Rome made further demands, including that the Carthaginians should evacuate their city altogether and move inland sixteen kilometers from the coast. This was not only a huge inconvenience but an outright ploy to steal the lucrative coastal city and take over Carthaginian trade. If the merchants and fishermen of Carthage were moved inland, their entire community's economy would collapse.

Chapter Thirty-Six - 149-146 BCE

The Siege of Carthage

In 149 BCE, Roman senator Cato the Elder dictated that Carthage was still beholden to Rome for the transgressions of the First and Second Punic Wars and was, therefore, under the authority of the Republic.[136] Carthage could not consent to Rome's demands, however, so the republic decided to destroy the city altogether.

Desiring to have the former capital of the Carthaginian Empire rebuilt further inland, Rome sent an embassy to the conquered city to make arrangements. The Senate demanded that Carthage be deconstructed and moved, but of course, the residents refused to take part. Once more at odds with one another, Carthage and Rome engaged in war—the Third Punic War, which was waged from 149 to 146 BCE.[137]

The Roman consuls Marcius Censorinus and Manius Manilius commanded the army and prepared for a long siege. As many as 80,000 infantrymen and 4,000 cavalry soldiers were sent to their

---

[136] Mark, Joshua. "Carthage." *Ancient History Encyclopedia*. Web. 2018.

[137] Ibid.

command in North Africa.[138] As for Carthage, it prepared for war by releasing its slaves from the city and recalling 30,000 soldiers back from Numidia.[139] In all, Carthage had about 230,000 citizens preparing for battle when the Romans marched up to the city walls.

The Carthaginians were well-prepared, their city already boasting about thirty-four kilometers of defensive walls, some in triple layers. There were ditches, palisades, walls, and even the sea itself to keep out the invading forces, and for a long time, the Roman army failed to make any significant headway. Though the consuls strategically moved to blockade the city's main port, they were unable to do so effectively. Merchant vessels were often quite able to maneuver the blockading ships and resupply Carthage with food, weapons, and ammunition.

Furthermore, Carthaginian forces did not just sit in defensive positions but made attacks on blockaders whenever the conditions were right. They set their own ships ablaze and let them drift out to the Roman ships, putting fire to the entire fleet. Roman siege engines, in the form of catapults and other destructive equipment, were targeted constantly by the city defenders. It was looking bad for Rome, and then, in the summer of 148 BCE, things became even worse when sickness broke through the invading ranks.[140]

The situation became direr when the Numidians, under the orders of the new king, Bithyas, sent 800 cavalrymen to join the Carthaginian ranks against Rome.[141] The siege continued, but with limited success, until the new consul, Publius Cornelius Scipio Aemilianus, stepped in to command the Roman army in 147 BCE.[142] Scipio was

---

[138] Cartwright, Mark. "Third Punic War." *Ancient History Encyclopedia*. Web. 2016.

[139] Ibid.

[140] Ibid.

[141] Ibid.

[142] Cartwright, Mark. "Third Punic War." *Ancient History Encyclopedia*. Web. 2016.

young, strong, and ambitious, and under his direction, the Romans slowly gripped Carthage in their control.

The first task was to construct a better siege wall around the city and its harbor from which the Roman soldiers could attack from high ground or shrink back behind the defenses when necessary. The offensive wall featured a mole—that is, a sturdy makeshift pier—on the south side by which soldiers could be evacuated or sent in. The mole had another role to play, which was to hem in the Carthaginian port that had thus far never been properly blockaded. With the mole positioned to block access, the Carthaginians were unable to receive further supplies by sea. They attempted to break through and establish a secondary channel, but the Romans beat them back.

With Carthage protected by its vast defensive system, its army had been mobile between several smaller communities, engaging Rome on land multiple times. Scipio took advantage of this once his siege walls had been constructed, however, and held the bulk of the army engaged at the city of Nepheris, twenty-five kilometers south of Carthage, while the remainder of his own men led a vicious attack from the mole. After a siege that lasted three weeks, Scipio took Nepheris and turned back to Carthage.

Month by month, the Romans gained ground and eventually overran the city by the spring of 146 BCE.[143] By the time they broke through Carthage's defenses, they had been laying siege to the city for a total of three years. Once the Roman army broke through, its ranks flooded it and sacked the city, leaving nothing undamaged. For seven whole days, the invading army fought one-on-one in the streets of the city, looting and destroying everything in sight. Hasdrubal and his family hid in the temple of Eshmun, along with 900 Roman deserters.[144] With only the citadel of Carthage left to be overtaken, Hasdrubal surrendered. His wife, however, chose to

---

[143] Ibid.

[144] Ibid.

sacrifice her children and then herself on the funeral pyre rather than be taken into enemy custody. The survivors were taken into Scipio's custody, and when the ransacking was done, the consul ordered the remains of the city to be burned so thoroughly that it was unrecognizable as the once-great city it had been for so long.

Epilogue

In the late stages of the Siege of Carthage, many inhabitants of the city died from starvation, if not from hand-to-hand combat, in that final week. When it was all over, 50,000 surviving Carthaginians were taken prisoner by the Roman legions and ultimately sold as slaves.[145] The Carthaginian Empire virtually extinguished, the Roman Republic moved in and systematically rebuilt the great African cities as part of its own expanded territory. Everything that had been under Carthaginian control now belonged to Rome. Scipio the Younger was given the additional name Africanus in celebration of his decisive victory in Africa.

Plutarch had this to say of the famous general and consul, who died in 129 BCE under suspicious circumstances:

"The Younger Scipio, they say, in the fifty-four years of his life bought nothing, sold nothing, built nothing, and left only thirty-three pounds of silver and two of gold in a great estate. So little he left, in spite of the fact that he was master of Carthage, and was the one among the generals who had made his soldiers richest."

---

[145] Scullard, Howard Hayes. *A History of the Roman World, 753 to 146 BC.* 2002.

Though legends persist about the Romans sowing the African soil with salt, the truth is that the annexed land was shared between Italian and local farmers. Grain was planted there and flourished, and Africa soon became one of the great cereal producers of the Roman Republic. Many Carthaginian cities were rebuilt in the Roman fashion, making the transfer of power physically and culturally complete. Utica, which had notably changed its allegiance during the Roman siege, was made the capital of the Roman province of Africa.

In Rome and Italy, the result of the three Punic Wars was a reduction in the number of people living in the countryside. So many men had gone to war, and many of those had died or never returned. People left their farms looking for work in the capital, which they found in the form of the army industry. People who had never seen the city before were overawed at its size, its festivals, its goods, and its industries, and more and more flocked to join the urban sprawl.

When the wars ended, one after another, returning veterans often decided to settle in Rome instead of going back to farming. This left swathes of farmland available for low prices so that industrious landowners could buy it up in huge tracts, setting up immense crops in place of household gardens and humble patches of grain. Many of Italy's cities swelled in size, and Rome became the most populous city in Europe.

The central trade and transport hub for Roman Africa's precious resources would eventually be none other than Roman Carthage, the city rebuilt by Julius Caesar in the 1st century on the same land the Romans had razed so determinedly 200 years earlier.[146]

---

[146] Stanley D. Brunn, Maureen Hays-Mitchell, Donald J. Zeigler (eds.). *Cities of the World: World Regional Urban Development*. 2012.

Here's another book by Captivating History that you might be interested in

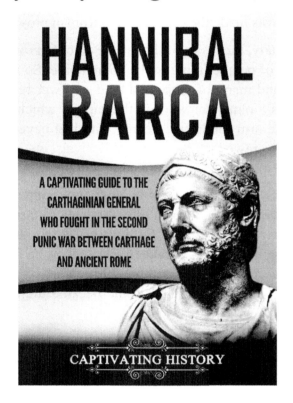

Printed in Great Britain
by Amazon

11164006R00079